THE SUPER EASY
SLOW COOKER
COOKBOOK

FROM BREAKFASTS TO DRINKS
FOR BUSY PEOPLE

ANDY FOSTER

COPYRIGHT NOTICE

© 2024 by Andy Foster. All rights reserved.

This book, including all its content such as recipes, photographs, illustrations, and text, is protected by international copyright laws.

No part of this publication may be reproduced, distributed, or transmitted in any form or by any means, including photocopying, recording, or other electronic or mechanical methods, without the prior written permission of the author and publisher, except in the case of brief quotations embodied in critical reviews and certain non-commercial uses permitted by copyright law.

For permission requests, please contact the publisher in writing.
The author and publisher have made every effort to ensure the accuracy and completeness of the information; however, they assume no responsibility for errors, omissions, or contrary interpretations.

The recipes, methods, and techniques described in this book are for home use only and are not intended for any commercial use or professional culinary applications without explicit authorization from the copyright holder.

Any unauthorized use, including but not limited to reproduction, modification, distribution, or republication of the material for commercial purposes, without prior written consent, is strictly prohibited and may result in legal action.

By purchasing this book, you agree to the terms of this copyright notice.
For permissions, inquiries, or further information, please contact the author or publisher.

CONTENTS

BEFORE YOU START	4
BREAKFASTS	7
SOUPS	15
STEWS	23
MEAT AND POULTRY	31
FISH AND SEAFOOD	39
VEGETABLES AND SIDES	47
BEANS AND GRAINS	55
SAUCES AND DIPS	63
DESSERTS	71
DRINKS	79
CONCLUSION	86

BEFORE YOU START
USEFUL TIPS AND RECOMMENDATIONS

- **Pre-sear the meat:**
Searing the meat before adding it to the slow cooker helps seal in the juices and create a crust that adds depth of flavor. This is especially important for lean meats, which can become dry. Additionally, browned meat gives the dish a more appetizing aroma.

- **Don't open the lid:**
Each time you lift the lid, a significant amount of heat escapes, which can extend the cooking time by 20–30 minutes. Try to check the dish only when necessary. Trust the timer and your slow cooker settings.

- **Vegetables at the bottom:**
Root vegetables like carrots or potatoes take longer to cook than meat. Place them at the bottom of the slow cooker, closer to the heat source. This ensures even cooking of all the ingredients.

- **Proper filling:**
Don't overfill the slow cooker. Ideally, fill it to 50–75% to allow for proper heat circulation. This ensures a stable internal temperature and more even cooking.

- **Ensure even cooking:**
Cut ingredients into equal-sized pieces so they cook evenly. Large chunks may remain undercooked, while smaller ones can overcook. This is especially important when cooking meat and vegetables together.

- **Gradual spice addition:**
Spices and herbs lose their flavor when exposed to long heat. It's better to add them closer to the end of cooking to preserve their aroma. If your dish needs strong flavors, use ground spices, while whole ones can be added at the beginning.

- **Use onions and garlic for aroma:**
Onions and garlic release their aromas over long cooking times. They add sweetness and depth of flavor to your dish. You can sauté them before adding to the slow cooker to enhance the aroma.

- **Thickeners at the end:**
If your dish is too watery, add thickeners like flour or cornstarch at the end. This will prevent clumping and give you more control over the sauce's consistency. Simply dissolve the flour in water and gradually add it to the dish.

BEFORE YOU START
USEFUL TIPS AND RECOMMENDATIONS

- **Freeze cooked meals:**
The slow cooker allows you to prepare large portions. Freeze the leftovers in containers to use as ready-made meals later. This is especially convenient for soups, stews, and casseroles.

- **Steam cooking:**
Some Crock-Pot models have a steamer function. Use it for cooking vegetables, fish, or even rice. It's a healthy and simple way to cook while preserving vitamins.

- **Use the timer:**
If your slow cooker has a timer, use it to control the cooking time. This prevents overcooking and makes the process easier. After the program ends, many models switch to a warm-keeping mode.

- **Switch to high heat to save time:**
If you're short on time, you can use the high-heat setting. However, keep in mind that this can affect the texture of the dish, making it denser or less tender.

- **Add greens at the end:**
To preserve the fresh flavor and bright color of greens, add them at the very end of cooking. This is especially important for fresh herbs like parsley or cilantro.

- **Slow-cooking beans:**
Soaking beans before cooking will reduce their cooking time in the slow cooker. They'll become soft and flavorful while maintaining their texture. This is especially important for beans, chickpeas, and lentils.

- **Make soups and broths overnight:**
Set your slow cooker on low and let it cook broth or soup overnight. By morning, you'll have a rich, flavorful broth. This saves time and allows ingredients to cook thoroughly.

- **Even flavor distribution:**
To ensure all ingredients soak up the spices and sauce, stir them before turning on the slow cooker. This helps evenly distribute the flavor throughout the dish.

- **Use dividers:**
If your model has dividers, you can cook several dishes at once without mixing them. This is convenient when you need to prepare both a side dish and a main course at the same time.

THE SUPER EASY SLOW COOKER COOKBOOK

BREAKFASTS

1. APPLE CINNAMON OATMEAL (OVERNIGHT OATS)
2. EGG, CHEESE, AND HAM CASSEROLE
3. BERRY AND NUT OATMEAL
4. COCONUT MILK RICE PORRIDGE
5. QUINOA PORRIDGE WITH FRUITS AND HONEY
6. VEGETABLE OMELETTE WITH CHEESE

BREAKFASTS
1. APPLE CINNAMON OATMEAL (OVERNIGHT OATS)

- Preparation Time: 10 minutes
- Cooking Time: 7-8 hours (overnight on low)
- Servings: 4-6

INGREDIENTS

- 2 cups steel-cut oats
- 4 cups water (or milk for a creamier texture)
- 1 1/2 cups unsweetened apple sauce (or 2 apples, peeled and chopped)
- 1/4 cup maple syrup or honey
- 1 teaspoon ground cinnamon
- 1/4 teaspoon ground nutmeg (optional)
- 1/4 teaspoon salt
- 1/2 teaspoon vanilla extract
- 1/4 cup raisins (optional)
- 1/4 cup chopped walnuts or pecans (optional)
- Additional toppings: sliced apples, nuts, more cinnamon, or a drizzle of honey

COOKING INSTRUCTIONS

1. Lightly grease the inside of the slow cooker with cooking spray or butter to prevent sticking.
2. Combine the steel-cut oats, water (or milk), applesauce (or chopped apples), maple syrup or honey, cinnamon, nutmeg, salt, and vanilla extract in the slow cooker. Stir everything together to evenly distribute the ingredients.
3. If you like a bit of extra texture, add raisins and chopped nuts to the mixture. Stir again to combine.
4. Cover the slow cooker and cook on low heat for 7-8 hours, allowing the oatmeal to cook overnight.
5. In the morning, give the oatmeal a good stir to combine everything. Serve the oatmeal warm with additional toppings like sliced apples, more nuts, or a drizzle of honey if desired.

SERVING TIPS AND VARIATIONS

- Serve the warm oatmeal with your favorite toppings such as fresh apple slices, chopped nuts, extra cinnamon, or a splash of milk. You can also sprinkle chia seeds or flaxseeds for added nutrition.
- Use almond milk, coconut milk, or another plant-based milk for a dairy-free option.
- Swap the apple sauce with pear sauce or mashed bananas for a different flavor profile.
- Add a tablespoon of chia seeds or flaxseeds before cooking for a thicker, fiber-rich texture.
- For extra flavor, add a pinch of ground cloves or allspice to the cinnamon and nutmeg mix.
- If you prefer a crunchy texture, toast some nuts in a skillet and add them right before serving.
- If using rolled oats instead of steel-cut oats, reduce the cooking time to 4-5 hours.

BREAKFASTS
2. EGG, CHEESE AND HAM CASSEROLE

- Preparation Time: 15 minutes
- Cooking Time: 2-3 hours on high or 4-6 hours on low
- Servings: 6-8

INGREDIENTS

- 12 large eggs
- 1 1/2 cups diced ham (cooked)
- 1 1/2 cups shredded cheddar cheese (or a mix of your favorite cheeses)
- 1/2 cup milk or cream
- 1/2 teaspoon garlic powder
- 1/2 teaspoon onion powder
- 1/2 teaspoon dried parsley
- Salt and pepper to taste
- 2 cups frozen hash browns or diced potatoes (optional)
- 1/2 cup diced bell peppers (optional)
- 1/2 cup diced onion (optional)
- Cooking spray or butter (for greasing the slow cooker)
- Fresh herbs for garnish (optional)

COOKING INSTRUCTIONS

1. Grease the inside of the slow cooker with cooking spray or butter to prevent the casserole from sticking.
2. In a large bowl, whisk together the eggs, milk or cream, garlic powder, onion powder, dried parsley, salt, and pepper until well combined.
3. If using hash browns or diced potatoes, place them at the bottom of the slow cooker. Then, layer the diced ham, bell peppers, and onion (if using). Pour the egg mixture over the top and sprinkle the shredded cheese evenly across the casserole.
4. Cover the slow cooker and cook on low heat for 4-6 hours or high heat for 2-3 hours, until the eggs are set and the casserole is fully cooked. The edges should be golden, and a toothpick inserted into the center should come out clean.
5. Once done, let the casserole cool slightly before slicing it into portions. Garnish with fresh herbs like parsley or chives, and serve hot.

SERVING TIPS AND VARIATIONS

- Serve this casserole as a hearty breakfast or brunch dish. It pairs well with toast, fresh fruit, or a light salad.
- Use different types of cheese such as Swiss, mozzarella, or pepper jack for varied flavors.
- Add a pinch of smoked paprika or red pepper flakes for a hint of spice.
- If you prefer a creamier texture, use half-and-half or heavy cream instead of milk.
- You can prepare this dish the night before and store it in the fridge. In the morning, simply turn on the slow cooker.

BREAKFASTS
3. BERRY AND NUT OATMEAL

- Preparation Time: 5 minutes
- Cooking Time: 6-8 hours on low (or 3-4 hours on high)
- Servings: 4-6

INGREDIENTS

- 1 ½ cups steel-cut oats
- 4 cups milk (or water, or a combination of both)
- 1 cup mixed berries (fresh or frozen; blueberries, strawberries, raspberries)
- 1/2 cup chopped nuts (such as almonds, walnuts, or pecans)
- 2 tablespoons honey or maple syrup (optional, for sweetness)
- 1 teaspoon vanilla extract
- 1 teaspoon cinnamon
- Pinch of salt
- Additional toppings: fresh berries, nuts, a drizzle of honey or maple syrup (optional)

COOKING INSTRUCTIONS

1. Lightly grease the inside of the slow cooker with cooking spray or butter to prevent the oatmeal from sticking.
2. In the slow cooker, combine the steel-cut oats, milk (or water), berries, chopped nuts, cinnamon, vanilla extract, and a pinch of salt. Stir well to mix the ingredients evenly.
3. Cover the slow cooker with the lid and cook on low heat for 6-8 hours (ideal for overnight) or on high heat for 3-4 hours if you need it ready faster. Stir occasionally, if possible, to prevent sticking and ensure even cooking.
4. When the oatmeal is cooked, it should be creamy, and the oats should be tender. If the mixture looks too thick, stir in a bit more milk or water until you reach your desired consistency.
5. If desired, stir in honey or maple syrup to sweeten the oatmeal, adjusting to your taste.
6. Once the oatmeal is ready, spoon it into bowls and add additional toppings such as fresh berries, extra nuts, or a drizzle of honey or maple syrup for an extra touch of flavor.

SERVING TIPS AND VARIATIONS

- Serve the oatmeal warm with a splash of milk, yogurt, or a sprinkle of granola for added texture.
- Use different fruits such as apples, pears, or bananas in place of berries.
- Experiment with different nuts or seeds like sunflower seeds or chia seeds.
- For a richer flavor, swap out some of the milk for coconut milk or almond milk.

BREAKFASTS
4. COCONUT MILK RICE PORRIDGE

- Preparation Time: 5 minutes
- Cooking Time: 2-3 hours on high or 4-6 hours on low
- Servings: 4-6

INGREDIENTS

- 1 cup jasmine rice (or any long-grain rice)
- 4 cups coconut milk (canned or carton)
- 1 ½ cups water
- 1/4 cup sugar or honey (adjust to taste)
- 1 teaspoon vanilla extract
- Pinch of salt
- Optional toppings: fresh fruit (mango, banana), shredded coconut, nuts, honey or maple syrup

COOKING INSTRUCTIONS

1. Lightly grease the inside of the slow cooker with cooking spray or butter to prevent sticking.
2. In the slow cooker, add the rice, coconut milk, water, sugar (or honey), vanilla extract, and a pinch of salt. Stir well to combine all the ingredients evenly.
3. Cover the slow cooker with the lid and cook on high heat for 2-3 hours or low heat for 4-6 hours, stirring occasionally to prevent the rice from clumping or sticking to the sides.
4. Once the rice is tender and the porridge has thickened to your liking, taste it for sweetness. If you prefer a thinner consistency, add more coconut milk or water and stir. Adjust sweetness if needed.
5. Ladle the warm coconut milk rice porridge into bowls and top with your favorite toppings like fresh fruit, shredded coconut, nuts, or a drizzle of honey or maple syrup for added flavor.

SERVING TIPS AND VARIATIONS

- Serve warm for breakfast, dessert, or a comforting snack. You can also refrigerate leftovers and serve chilled with fresh fruit.
- Add a touch of spice by stirring in ground cinnamon, cardamom, or ginger.
- For added texture, mix in cooked quinoa or chia seeds.
- Try using brown rice for a nuttier flavor, but increase cooking time by 1-2 hours.
- Swap some of the coconut milk for almond milk or regular milk for a different flavor profile.

BREAKFASTS
5. QUINOA PORRIDGE WITH FRUITS AND HONEY

- Preparation Time: 5 minutes
- Cooking Time: 2-3 hours on high or 4-5 hours on low
- Servings: 4

INGREDIENTS

- 1 cup quinoa, rinsed
- 3 cups almond milk (or any milk of your choice)
- 1 teaspoon vanilla extract
- 2 tablespoons honey (adjust to taste)
- 1/2 teaspoon cinnamon (optional)
- Pinch of salt
- 1 cup mixed fruits (fresh or dried, such as berries, bananas, apples, or raisins)
- Optional toppings: chopped nuts, extra honey, fresh fruit, shredded coconut

COOKING INSTRUCTIONS

1. Lightly grease the inside of the slow cooker with cooking spray or butter to prevent sticking.
2. In the slow cooker, combine the rinsed quinoa, almond milk, honey, vanilla extract, cinnamon (if using), and a pinch of salt. Stir well to mix the ingredients evenly.
3. Cover the slow cooker with the lid and cook on high heat for 2-3 hours or low heat for 4-5 hours, stirring occasionally to ensure the quinoa cooks evenly and absorbs the liquid.
4. Once the quinoa is tender and the porridge has thickened, taste it for sweetness. You can add more honey if desired. If the porridge is too thick, stir in a little more milk to reach your desired consistency.
5. About 30 minutes before the porridge is finished cooking, stir in the mixed fruits. For fresh fruits like berries or bananas, you can also add them right before serving to maintain their texture.
6. Spoon the warm quinoa porridge into bowls and top with extra honey, fresh fruit, chopped nuts, or shredded coconut for added flavor and texture.

SERVING TIPS AND VARIATIONS

- Serve warm for breakfast or a hearty snack. You can also refrigerate leftovers and enjoy chilled or reheated with additional toppings.
- Swap almond milk for coconut milk or regular milk for a creamier porridge.
- Use maple syrup instead of honey for a different flavor.
- Add dried fruits like raisins or apricots for added texture.
- For a richer flavor, add a dollop of yogurt or a drizzle of nut butter on top before serving.

BREAKFASTS
6. VEGETABLE OMELETTE WITH CHEESE

- Preparation Time: 10 minutes
- Cooking Time: 2-3 hours on low
- Servings: 4-6

INGREDIENTS

- 8 large eggs
- 1 cup milk (or cream for a richer omelette)
- 1 ½ cups shredded cheese (cheddar, mozzarella, or your favorite cheese)
- 1 small onion, diced
- 1 bell pepper, diced
- 1 zucchini, diced
- 1 cup mushrooms, sliced
- 1 cup spinach, chopped
- Salt and pepper to taste
- 1/2 teaspoon garlic powder (optional)
- 1/2 teaspoon paprika (optional)

COOKING INSTRUCTIONS

1. Lightly grease the inside of the slow cooker with cooking spray or butter to prevent the omelette from sticking.
2. In a large mixing bowl, whisk together the eggs, milk, salt, pepper, garlic powder, and paprika. Make sure the mixture is well combined.
3. Stir in the diced onion, bell pepper, zucchini, mushrooms, and spinach. Mix in 1 cup of the shredded cheese, reserving the remaining 1/2 cup for topping later.
4. Pour the egg and vegetable mixture into the slow cooker. Spread it evenly with a spatula.
5. Cover the slow cooker with the lid and cook on low heat for 2-3 hours, or until the eggs are set and the center is firm. The cooking time may vary depending on your slow cooker.
6. About 10 minutes before the omelette is done, sprinkle the remaining 1/2 cup of shredded cheese on top. Cover and let the cheese melt completely.
7. Use a toothpick or knife to check the center of the omelette. If it comes out clean, the omelette is ready to serve.
8. Once cooked, turn off the slow cooker and allow the omelette to cool slightly before slicing and serving.

SERVING TIPS AND VARIATIONS

- Serve warm with toast, avocado, or a side of fresh salad for a complete meal.
- Add cooked bacon, ham, or sausage for a meaty version.
- Experiment with different vegetables like tomatoes, broccoli, or asparagus.
- Use different cheeses such as feta, goat cheese, or Swiss for varied flavors.
- Add fresh herbs like parsley, chives, or basil for extra freshness.

SOUPS

1. **CHICKEN NOODLE SOUP**
2. **PUMPKIN CREAM SOUP**
3. **MUSHROOM SOUP WITH POTATOES**
4. **BEAN AND SAUSAGE SOUP**
5. **BEEF VEGETABLE SOUP**
6. **BROCCOLI CHEESE SOUP**

SOUPS
1. CHICKEN NOODLE SOUP

- Preparation Time: 10 minutes
- Cooking Time: 6-8 hours on low or 3-4 hours on high
- Servings: 6-8

INGREDIENTS

- 1 ½ pounds boneless, skinless chicken breasts or thighs
- 8 cups chicken broth
- 3 medium carrots, peeled and sliced
- 2 celery stalks, sliced
- 1 small onion, diced
- 3 cloves garlic, minced
- 2 teaspoons dried thyme
- 1 teaspoon dried oregano
- 1 bay leaf
- Salt and pepper to taste
- 8 ounces egg noodles (or pasta of your choice)
- 2 tablespoons fresh parsley, chopped (optional, for garnish)
- Juice of 1 lemon (optional, for added freshness)

COOKING INSTRUCTIONS

1. Lightly grease the inside of the slow cooker or simply add the ingredients to the slow cooker.
2. Place the chicken breasts or thighs into the slow cooker. Add the sliced carrots, celery, diced onion, and minced garlic on top.
3. Sprinkle the dried thyme, oregano, and salt and pepper over the vegetables. Add the bay leaf. Pour the chicken broth into the slow cooker, ensuring the chicken and vegetables are fully submerged.
4. Cover the slow cooker with the lid and cook on low heat for 6-8 hours or high heat for 3-4 hours until the chicken is fully cooked and tender.
5. Once the chicken is cooked, remove it from the slow cooker and shred it using two forks. Return the shredded chicken to the slow cooker.
6. About 30 minutes before serving, add the egg noodles (or pasta) to the slow cooker. Stir well and cook until the noodles are tender.
7. Before serving, remove the bay leaf and stir in the fresh parsley and lemon juice if desired. Taste and adjust seasonings if needed.

SERVING TIPS AND VARIATIONS

- Serve the soup warm with a side of garlic bread or a simple salad. It's perfect for a comforting meal during colder months.
- For a creamier soup, stir in a splash of heavy cream or coconut milk before serving.
- Add other vegetables like peas, corn, or spinach for extra nutrition.
- Substitute the egg noodles with gluten-free pasta or whole-grain pasta for a healthier option.
- For added depth of flavor, sauté the onions, garlic, and celery in a little olive oil before adding them to the slow cooker.

SOUPS
2. PUMPKIN CREAM SOUP

- Preparation Time: 10 minutes
- Cooking Time: 6-8 hours on low or 3-4 hours on high
- Servings: 6-8

INGREDIENTS

- 1 can (15 oz) pumpkin puree (or 4 cups fresh pumpkin, peeled and cubed)
- 1 small onion, chopped
- 2 carrots, peeled and chopped
- 2 cloves garlic, minced
- 4 cups vegetable or chicken broth
- 1 cup heavy cream or coconut milk (for a dairy-free option)
- 1 teaspoon ground cinnamon
- ½ teaspoon ground nutmeg
- ½ teaspoon ground ginger
- 1 tablespoon maple syrup or honey (optional, for sweetness)
- Salt and pepper to taste
- 2 tablespoons olive oil or butter
- Fresh parsley, chopped (for garnish)

COOKING INSTRUCTIONS

1. Lightly grease the inside of the slow cooker with olive oil or butter.
2. In the slow cooker, combine the pumpkin puree (or cubed fresh pumpkin), chopped onion, carrots, garlic, vegetable or chicken broth, cinnamon, nutmeg, ginger, and a pinch of salt and pepper. Stir to combine.
3. Cover the slow cooker with the lid and cook on low heat for 6-8 hours or high heat for 3-4 hours, until the vegetables are tender.
4. Once the vegetables are fully cooked, use an immersion blender to blend the soup until smooth and creamy. Alternatively, transfer the soup in batches to a blender, then return it to the slow cooker.
5. Stir in the heavy cream (or coconut milk) and maple syrup or honey (if using). Taste and adjust the seasoning with more salt and pepper if needed.
6. Let the soup continue to cook for an additional 10-15 minutes on low heat to allow the cream to heat through.
7. Ladle the warm pumpkin cream soup into bowls. Garnish with fresh parsley and any optional toppings like croutons, pumpkin seeds, or a drizzle of cream or olive oil.

SERVING TIPS AND VARIATIONS

- Serve this creamy pumpkin soup with a side of crusty bread or a green salad for a complete meal. It also pairs well with grilled cheese sandwiches for a comforting lunch.
- Add a pinch of cayenne pepper or smoked paprika for a hint of heat.
- Use butternut squash or sweet potatoes in place of pumpkin for a different flavor.
- For a richer soup, use half heavy cream and half cream cheese for a more decadent texture.
- Top with crispy bacon bits or sautéed mushrooms for added texture and flavor.

SOUPS
3. MUSHROOM SOUP WITH POTATOES

- Preparation Time: 10 minutes
- Cooking Time: 6-8 hours on low or 3-4 hours on high
- Servings: 6-8

INGREDIENTS

- 1 pound (450g) mushrooms (such as cremini, button, or a mix), sliced
- 4 medium potatoes, peeled and diced
- 1 medium onion, chopped
- 3 cloves garlic, minced
- 4 cups vegetable or chicken broth
- 1 cup heavy cream or half-and-half
- 2 tablespoons olive oil or butter
- 1 teaspoon dried thyme
- 1 bay leaf
- Salt and pepper to taste
- 1 tablespoon flour (optional, to thicken)
- Fresh parsley, chopped (for garnish)
- Optional toppings: croutons, grated Parmesan cheese or a drizzle of olive oil

COOKING INSTRUCTIONS

1. Lightly grease the inside of the slow cooker with olive oil or butter.
2. For extra flavor, sauté the sliced mushrooms and onions in a skillet with olive oil or butter over medium heat for 5-7 minutes until the mushrooms release their liquid and the onions soften. This step is optional but adds depth to the soup.
3. Add the diced potatoes, sautéed mushrooms (or raw mushrooms), onions, garlic, thyme, and bay leaf to the slow cooker. Pour in the broth and stir to combine. Season with salt and pepper to taste.
4. Cover the slow cooker with the lid and cook on low heat for 6-8 hours or high heat for 3-4 hours, until the potatoes are tender and the flavors have melded together.
5. If you prefer a thicker soup, whisk 1 tablespoon of flour with a small amount of broth or water to make a slurry. Stir the slurry into the soup about 30 minutes before serving, and let it cook to thicken.
6. About 15-20 minutes before serving, stir in the heavy cream or half-and-half. Let the soup heat through.
7. Once the soup is fully cooked, remove the bay leaf and ladle the soup into bowls.

SERVING TIPS AND VARIATIONS

- Serve the mushroom and potato soup with crusty bread or garlic bread for a satisfying meal.
- Use a mix of wild mushrooms for a deeper, earthier flavor.
- Add chopped carrots or celery for extra texture and flavor.
- For a creamier version, blend a portion of the soup with an immersion blender and then stir it back into the pot.
- Swap the heavy cream with coconut milk for a dairy-free version.

SOUPS
4. BEAN AND SAUSAGE SOUP

- Preparation Time: 10 minutes
- Cooking Time: 6-8 hours on low or 3-4 hours on high
- Servings: 6-8

INGREDIENTS

- 1 pound (450g) smoked sausage or chorizo, sliced
- 2 cans (15 oz each) white beans (such as cannellini or navy beans), drained and rinsed
- 1 can (15 oz) diced tomatoes
- 1 medium onion, diced
- 2 carrots, peeled and sliced
- 2 celery stalks, sliced
- 3 cloves garlic, minced
- 4 cups chicken or vegetable broth
- 1 teaspoon dried thyme
- 1 teaspoon smoked paprika (optional)
- 1 bay leaf
- Salt and pepper to taste
- 2 tablespoons olive oil
- Fresh parsley, chopped (for garnish)

COOKING INSTRUCTIONS

1. Lightly grease the inside of the slow cooker with olive oil or simply add all ingredients directly.
2. For extra flavor, heat the olive oil in a skillet over medium heat and brown the sliced sausage for 3-4 minutes until lightly crisped. This step is optional but enhances the flavor.
3. In the slow cooker, add the browned sausage (if cooked), white beans, diced tomatoes, onions, carrots, celery, garlic, thyme, smoked paprika (if using), bay leaf, and broth. Stir well to combine.
4. Add salt and pepper to taste, but remember that the sausage may already be salty. Adjust the seasoning later if needed.
5. Cover the slow cooker with the lid and cook on low heat for 6-8 hours or high heat for 3-4 hours, until the vegetables are tender and the flavors have melded together.
6. Before serving, remove the bay leaf and taste the soup. Adjust the seasoning with additional salt, pepper, or smoked paprika if needed.
7. Ladle the soup into bowls and garnish with freshly chopped parsley. You can also top it with grated Parmesan cheese or croutons for added texture and flavor.

SERVING TIPS AND VARIATIONS

- Serve the soup warm with crusty bread or a side of garlic toast for a hearty meal.
- Use kielbasa, Italian sausage, or even cooked bacon instead of smoked sausage.
- Add spinach or kale for an extra boost of greens.
- For a thicker soup, mash some of the beans before adding them to the slow cooker.
- Swap white beans for black beans or kidney beans for a different flavor and texture.
- Add red pepper flakes or hot sauce for a spicy kick.

SOUPS
5. BEEF VEGETABLE SOUP

- Preparation Time: 15 minutes
- Cooking Time: 8-10 hours on low or 4-6 hours on high
- Servings: 6-8

INGREDIENTS

- 1 ½ pounds beef stew meat, cut into bite-sized pieces
- 4 cups beef broth
- 1 can (15 oz) diced tomatoes
- 3 medium potatoes, peeled and diced
- 2 medium carrots, peeled and sliced
- 2 celery stalks, sliced
- 1 medium onion, diced
- 2 cloves garlic, minced
- 1 cup frozen green beans (or fresh)
- 1 cup frozen peas
- 1 teaspoon dried thyme
- 1 teaspoon dried oregano
- 1 bay leaf
- 2 tablespoons tomato paste
- 1 tablespoon olive oil (optional, for browning the meat)
- Salt and pepper to taste

COOKING INSTRUCTIONS

1. Lightly grease the inside of the slow cooker or simply add all ingredients directly.
2. For enhanced flavor, heat the olive oil in a skillet over medium-high heat. Season the beef stew meat with salt and pepper, then brown the meat on all sides for 5-6 minutes. This step is optional but adds depth to the flavor of the soup. Transfer the browned beef to the slow cooker.
3. To the slow cooker, add the diced potatoes, carrots, celery, onion, garlic, and green beans. Pour in the beef broth and diced tomatoes (including their juice). Stir in the tomato paste, thyme, oregano, and bay leaf. Season with salt and pepper to taste.
4. Cover the slow cooker and cook on low heat for 8-10 hours or high heat for 4-6 hours, until the beef is tender and the vegetables are cooked through.
5. About 30 minutes before the soup is finished, stir in the frozen peas. Let the soup continue cooking to heat the peas through.
6. Before serving, remove the bay leaf and taste the soup. Adjust seasoning if needed with additional salt and pepper.
7. Ladle the warm beef vegetable soup into bowls and garnish with freshly chopped parsley. Serve with crusty bread or crackers.

SERVING TIPS AND VARIATIONS

- Pair this hearty soup with a green salad or a side of garlic bread for a complete meal.
- Add other vegetables like corn, zucchini, or bell peppers for more variety.
- Use sweet potatoes instead of regular potatoes for a sweeter, more nutrient-dense version.
- For a spicier soup, add a pinch of red pepper flakes or a diced jalapeño.
- Use different cuts of beef like chuck roast or shank for a richer broth.

SOUPS
6. BROCCOLI CHEESE SOUP

- Preparation Time: 10 minutes
- Cooking Time: 4-6 hours on low or 2-3 hours on high
- Servings: 6-8

INGREDIENTS

- 4 cups fresh broccoli florets (or frozen)
- 1 medium onion, chopped
- 2 cloves garlic, minced
- 4 cups chicken or vegetable broth
- 2 cups shredded sharp cheddar cheese
- 1 cup heavy cream or half-and-half
- 1 cup shredded carrots
- 2 tablespoons butter
- 1 tablespoon olive oil
- 2 tablespoons all-purpose flour
- 1 teaspoon Dijon mustard (optional)
- ½ teaspoon paprika
- Salt and pepper to taste
- Fresh parsley or extra cheese for garnish (optional)

COOKING INSTRUCTIONS

1. Lightly grease the inside of the slow cooker with butter or olive oil to prevent sticking.
2. In a skillet, heat the olive oil and butter over medium heat. Sauté the chopped onion and minced garlic for 3-4 minutes until softened. This step is optional but adds more flavor. Transfer the sautéed mixture to the slow cooker.
3. Add the broccoli florets and shredded carrots to the slow cooker.
4. Pour in the chicken or vegetable broth and stir in the paprika, Dijon mustard (if using), salt, and pepper.
5. Cover the slow cooker with the lid and cook on low heat for 4-6 hours or high heat for 2-3 hours, until the broccoli is tender.
6. About 30 minutes before serving, whisk together the flour and heavy cream (or half-and-half) in a small bowl. Stir this mixture into the slow cooker to thicken the soup.
7. Stir in the shredded cheddar cheese, making sure it melts evenly into the soup. Continue cooking for another 15-20 minutes on low heat, stirring occasionally, until the soup is smooth and creamy.
8. Once the soup is fully cooked and the cheese has melted, ladle the warm broccoli cheese soup into bowls. Garnish with extra cheese, fresh parsley, or croutons if desired.

SERVING TIPS AND VARIATIONS

- Serve with crusty bread, garlic bread, or a side salad for a complete meal. This soup also pairs well with a baked potato or roasted vegetables.
- Add cooked bacon or ham for a meaty version of the soup.
- Swap cheddar cheese with Swiss, gouda, or a mix of cheeses for a different flavor profile.
- Use frozen broccoli for convenience or add other vegetables like cauliflower or zucchini.
- For a thicker soup, blend half of the soup using an immersion blender and stir it back in.

THE SUPER EASY SLOW COOKER COOKBOOK

STEWS

1. BEEF STEWED IN RED WINE
2. CHICKEN STEW WITH POTATOES AND CARROTS
3. LAMB STEW WITH POTATOES AND ROSEMARY
4. SMOKED SAUSAGE AND BEAN STEW
5. VEAL IN CREAMY MUSHROOM SAUCE
6. BEEF BOURGUIGNON

STEWS
1. BEEF STEWED IN RED WINE

- Preparation Time: 15 minutes
- Cooking Time: 8-10 hours on low or 4-6 hours on high
- Servings: 6-8

INGREDIENTS

- 2 pounds beef stew meat, cut into bite-sized pieces
- 2 cups red wine (such as Cabernet Sauvignon or Merlot)
- 2 cups beef broth
- 2 medium carrots, peeled and sliced
- 1 large onion, chopped
- 3 cloves garlic, minced
- 2 tablespoons tomato paste
- 1 tablespoon olive oil (for browning, optional)
- 1 tablespoon flour (for thickening, optional)
- 1 teaspoon dried thyme
- 1 teaspoon dried rosemary
- 2 bay leaves
- Salt and pepper to taste
- Fresh parsley, chopped (for garnish)

COOKING INSTRUCTIONS

1. Lightly grease the inside of the slow cooker or simply add the ingredients directly.
2. Heat the olive oil in a skillet over medium-high heat. Season the beef with salt and pepper, then brown the meat in batches for 4-5 minutes until seared on all sides. This step is optional but adds flavor. Transfer the browned beef to the slow cooker.
3. Add the chopped carrots, onions, and minced garlic to the slow cooker. Stir in the tomato paste, thyme, rosemary, and bay leaves.
4. Pour the red wine and beef broth over the beef and vegetables. Stir to combine.
5. Cover the slow cooker and cook on low heat for 8-10 hours or high heat for 4-6 hours, until the beef is tender and the flavors have developed.
6. If you'd like a thicker sauce, whisk 1 tablespoon of flour with a small amount of water to make a slurry. Stir the slurry into the stew about 30 minutes before serving, allowing it to thicken as it continues to cook.
7. Once the stew is done cooking, taste and adjust seasoning with additional salt and pepper if needed. Remove the bay leaves before serving.
8. Ladle the beef stew into bowls and garnish with freshly chopped parsley. Serve with crusty bread or over mashed potatoes, rice, or egg noodles.

SERVING TIPS AND VARIATIONS

- This rich and flavorful stew pairs well with mashed potatoes, buttered noodles, or crusty bread to soak up the sauce. A green salad or roasted vegetables also make great sides.
- Add vegetables like mushrooms, potatoes, or parsnips for extra heartiness.
- Use a mixture of herbs such as oregano or bay leaves for added flavor.
- For a deeper flavor, substitute half of the beef broth with additional red wine.

STEWS
2. CHICKEN STEW WITH POTATOES AND CARROTS

- Preparation Time: 15 minutes
- Cooking Time: 6-8 hours on low or 3-4 hours on high
- Servings: 6-8

INGREDIENTS

- 1 ½ pounds boneless, skinless chicken thighs or breasts, cut into bite-sized pieces
- 4 medium potatoes, peeled and diced
- 4 medium carrots, peeled and sliced
- 1 large onion, chopped
- 3 cloves garlic, minced
- 4 cups chicken broth
- 1 tablespoon tomato paste
- 2 teaspoons dried thyme
- 1 teaspoon dried rosemary
- 1 bay leaf
- Salt and pepper to taste
- 2 tablespoons olive oil (optional, for browning)
- 2 tablespoons all-purpose flour (optional, for thickening)
- Fresh parsley, chopped (for garnish)

COOKING INSTRUCTIONS

1. Lightly grease the inside of the slow cooker, or simply add the ingredients directly.
2. For extra flavor, heat olive oil in a skillet over medium-high heat. Season the chicken with salt and pepper, then brown the chicken pieces for 4-5 minutes until lightly golden on all sides. This step is optional but enhances the flavor. Transfer the browned chicken to the slow cooker.
3. Add the diced potatoes, sliced carrots, chopped onion, and minced garlic to the slow cooker. Stir in the tomato paste, thyme, rosemary, and bay leaf.
4. Pour the chicken broth over the ingredients in the slow cooker. Stir everything to combine well.
5. Cover the slow cooker and cook on low heat for 6-8 hours or high heat for 3-4 hours, until the chicken is tender and the vegetables are fully cooked.
6. If you prefer a thicker stew, whisk 2 tablespoons of flour with a small amount of water to make a slurry. Stir the slurry into the stew about 30 minutes before serving, and let it cook on low heat until it thickens.
7. Before serving, taste the stew and adjust seasoning with additional salt and pepper if needed. Remove the bay leaf before serving.
8. Ladle the chicken stew into bowls and garnish with freshly chopped parsley. Serve with crusty bread, rice, or a side salad for a complete meal.

SERVING TIPS AND VARIATIONS

- This hearty stew pairs well with crusty bread, biscuits, or a side of mashed potatoes. A green salad or roasted vegetables complement the meal perfectly.
- Add extra vegetables like celery, peas, or mushrooms for more variety.
- Use sweet potatoes instead of regular potatoes for a slightly sweeter and more nutritious dish.
- Substitute the chicken with turkey or pork for a different twist.

STEWS
3. LAMB STEW WITH POTATOES AND ROSEMARY

- Preparation Time: 15 minutes
- Cooking Time: 6-8 hours on low or 3-4 hours on high
- Servings: 6-8

INGREDIENTS

- 2 pounds lamb stew meat, cut into bite-sized pieces
- 4 medium potatoes, peeled and diced
- 3 medium carrots, peeled and sliced
- 1 large onion, chopped
- 3 cloves garlic, minced
- 3 cups beef or lamb broth
- 1 tablespoon tomato paste
- 2 tablespoons olive oil (optional, for browning)
- 1 tablespoon fresh rosemary, chopped (or 1 teaspoon dried rosemary)
- 1 teaspoon dried thyme
- 1 bay leaf
- Salt and pepper to taste
- 1 tablespoon flour (optional, for thickening)
- Fresh parsley, chopped (for garnish)

COOKING INSTRUCTIONS

1. Lightly grease the inside of the slow cooker or simply add the ingredients directly.
2. Heat olive oil in a skillet over medium-high heat. Season the lamb with salt and pepper. Brown the lamb in batches for 5-6 minutes, until seared on all sides. This step is optional but adds depth of flavor. Transfer the browned lamb to the slow cooker.
3. Add the diced potatoes, sliced carrots, chopped onion, and minced garlic to the slow cooker.
4. Pour the broth into the slow cooker. Stir in the tomato paste, rosemary, thyme, and bay leaf. Season with additional salt and pepper to taste.
5. Cover the slow cooker with the lid and cook on low heat for 6-8 hours or high heat for 3-4 hours, until the lamb is tender and the vegetables are cooked through.
6. If you'd like a thicker stew, whisk 1 tablespoon of flour with a small amount of water to make a slurry. Stir the slurry into the stew about 30 minutes before serving and allow it to thicken as it finishes cooking.
7. Once the stew is fully cooked, remove the bay leaf. Taste the stew and adjust seasoning with more salt, pepper, or rosemary as needed.
8. Ladle the lamb stew into bowls and garnish with freshly chopped parsley. Serve with crusty bread, mashed potatoes, or buttered noodles.

SERVING TIPS AND VARIATIONS

- This stew pairs beautifully with crusty bread, polenta, or couscous. It also goes well with a green salad or roasted vegetables.
- Add parsnips or sweet potatoes for extra flavor and variety.
- Use white wine instead of broth for a lighter flavor.
- Add peas or spinach in the last 15 minutes for a fresh, green element.

STEWS
4. SMOKED SAUSAGE AND BEAN STEW

- Preparation Time: 10 minutes
- Cooking Time: 6-8 hours on low or 3-4 hours on high
- Servings: 6-8

INGREDIENTS

- 1 pound smoked sausage, sliced
- 2 cans (15 oz each) kidney beans, drained and rinsed
- 1 can (14.5 oz) diced tomatoes
- 1 large onion, chopped
- 2 medium carrots, peeled and sliced
- 2 celery stalks, sliced
- 3 cloves garlic, minced
- 4 cups chicken broth
- 2 tablespoons tomato paste
- 1 teaspoon smoked paprika
- 1 teaspoon dried thyme
- 1 bay leaf
- Salt and pepper to taste
- 2 tablespoons olive oil (optional, for sautéing)
- Fresh parsley, chopped (for garnish)

COOKING INSTRUCTIONS

1. Lightly grease the inside of the slow cooker or simply add the ingredients directly.
2. For added flavor, heat olive oil in a skillet over medium heat. Sauté the sliced sausage for 3-4 minutes until slightly browned. Remove and set aside. In the same skillet, sauté the chopped onion, garlic, carrots, and celery for 5 minutes until softened. This step is optional but enhances the flavor. Transfer the sausage and vegetables to the slow cooker.
3. Add the kidney beans, diced tomatoes, smoked paprika, thyme, and bay leaf to the slow cooker. Season with salt and pepper to taste.
4. Pour in the chicken broth and stir in the tomato paste until well combined.
5. Cover the slow cooker with the lid and cook on low heat for 6-8 hours or high heat for 3-4 hours, until the vegetables are tender and the flavors have melded together.
6. Before serving, remove the bay leaf. Taste the stew and adjust seasoning with additional salt and pepper if needed.
7. Ladle the sausage and bean stew into bowls and garnish with freshly chopped parsley. Serve with crusty bread or over rice for a complete meal.

SERVING TIPS AND VARIATIONS

- This hearty stew pairs well with cornbread, rice, or mashed potatoes. For a lighter meal, serve it with a side salad.
- Add other beans like black beans or white beans for variety.
- Use andouille or chorizo sausage for a spicier kick.
- For a vegetarian version, use plant-based sausage and vegetable broth.
- For a thicker stew, mash some of the beans or add a cornstarch slurry in the last 30 minutes of cooking.

STEWS
5. VEAL IN CREAMY MUSHROOM SAUCE

- Preparation Time: 15 minutes
- Cooking Time: 6-8 hours on low or 3-4 hours on high
- Servings: 6

INGREDIENTS

- 2 pounds veal stew meat or veal shoulder, cut into bite-sized pieces
- 1 pound mushrooms (button, cremini, or mixed), sliced
- 1 large onion, chopped
- 3 cloves garlic, minced
- 1 ½ cups beef or veal broth
- 1 cup heavy cream or sour cream
- 1 tablespoon Dijon mustard
- 2 tablespoons olive oil or butter (optional, for browning)
- 1 tablespoon flour (optional, for thickening)
- 1 teaspoon dried thyme
- 1 teaspoon dried rosemary
- Salt and pepper to taste
- Fresh parsley, chopped (for garnish)

COOKING INSTRUCTIONS

1. Lightly grease the inside of the slow cooker or simply add the ingredients directly.
2. For added flavor, heat olive oil or butter in a skillet over medium-high heat. Season the veal with salt and pepper, then brown the meat in batches for 4-5 minutes until golden on all sides. Transfer the browned veal to the slow cooker.
3. In the same skillet, sauté the sliced mushrooms, chopped onion, and garlic for about 5 minutes, until the vegetables are soft. This step is optional but enhances the flavor. Transfer the vegetables to the slow cooker.
4. Pour the beef or veal broth into the slow cooker. Stir in the Dijon mustard, thyme, rosemary, and a pinch of salt and pepper. Stir to combine.
5. Cover the slow cooker and cook on low heat for 6-8 hours or high heat for 3-4 hours, until the veal is tender.
6. About 30 minutes before serving, stir in the heavy cream or sour cream to create the creamy sauce. If you'd like a thicker sauce, whisk 1 tablespoon of flour with a small amount of water to create a slurry, and stir it into the sauce. Let the stew cook for an additional 30 minutes on low heat to thicken.
7. Before serving, taste the sauce and adjust seasoning with more salt, pepper, or herbs if needed.
8. Ladle the veal in creamy mushroom sauce over mashed potatoes, pasta, or rice. Garnish with freshly chopped parsley.

SERVING TIPS AND VARIATIONS

- This dish pairs beautifully with mashed potatoes, buttered noodles, or polenta. Serve it with roasted vegetables or a green salad on the side.
- For a lighter version, substitute half the cream with Greek yogurt or use half-and-half.

STEWS
6. BEEF BOURGUIGNON

- Preparation Time: 20 minutes
- Cooking Time: 8-10 hours on low or 4-5 hours on high
- Servings: 6-8

INGREDIENTS

- 2 ½ pounds beef stew meat or chuck roast, cut into bite-sized pieces
- 6 slices bacon, chopped
- 2 cups red wine (such as Burgundy, Pinot Noir, or Merlot)
- 2 cups beef broth
- 3 large carrots, peeled and sliced
- 1 large onion, chopped
- 3 cloves garlic, minced
- 1 pound mushrooms, sliced
- 1 tablespoon tomato paste
- 2 tablespoons all-purpose flour (optional, for thickening)
- 2 tablespoons olive oil or butter (optional, for browning)
- 1 teaspoon dried thyme
- 1 bay leaf, Salt and pepper to taste
- Fresh parsley, chopped (for garnish)

COOKING INSTRUCTIONS

1. Lightly grease the inside of the slow cooker or simply add the ingredients directly.
2. In a skillet over medium heat, cook the chopped bacon until crisp. Transfer the bacon to a plate, leaving the rendered fat in the skillet.
3. In the same skillet, add olive oil or butter (if needed) and brown the beef in batches for 4-5 minutes until seared on all sides. Season with salt and pepper. This step is optional but adds depth of flavor. Transfer the browned beef to the slow cooker.
4. In the same skillet, sauté the chopped onion, garlic, and sliced mushrooms for 5 minutes, until softened. Transfer the vegetables to the slow cooker.
5. Pour the red wine and beef broth into the slow cooker. Stir in the tomato paste, thyme, and bay leaf. Add the carrots and browned bacon. Season with additional salt and pepper to taste.
6. Cover the slow cooker and cook on low heat for 8-10 hours or high heat for 4-5 hours, until the beef is tender and the flavors have melded together.
7. If you'd like a thicker sauce, whisk 2 tablespoons of flour with a small amount of water to make a slurry. Stir the slurry into the stew during the last 30 minutes of cooking, allowing the sauce to thicken.
8. Before serving, taste the stew and adjust seasoning with additional salt, pepper, or thyme if needed. Remove the bay leaf.
9. Ladle the beef bourguignon into bowls and garnish with freshly chopped parsley. Serve with mashed potatoes, buttered noodles, or crusty bread.

SERVING TIPS AND VARIATIONS

- This rich, flavorful stew pairs beautifully with mashed potatoes, polenta, or buttered egg noodles. Serve it with a side of roasted vegetables or a green salad.

MEAT AND POULTRY

1. MEXICAN-STYLE PULLED PORK
2. BEEF IN MUSTARD HONEY SAUCE
3. BEEF STEWED WITH POTATOES AND CARROTS
4. SPICY LAMB CURRY
5. PORK WITH PINEAPPLES AND SOY SAUCE
6. CHICKEN WITH HONEY AND MUSTARD

MEAT AND POULTRY
1. MEXICAN-STYLE PULLED PORK

- Preparation Time: 15 minutes
- Cooking Time: 8-10 hours on low or 4-6 hours on high
- Servings: 8-10

INGREDIENTS

- 3-4 pounds pork shoulder (or pork butt), boneless
- 1 large onion, chopped
- 4 cloves garlic, minced
- 1 can (14.5 oz) diced tomatoes
- 1 cup orange juice
- 1/4 cup lime juice (about 2 limes)
- 1 tablespoon chili powder
- 1 tablespoon cumin
- 1 teaspoon smoked paprika
- 1 teaspoon dried oregano
- 1 teaspoon ground black pepper
- 1 teaspoon salt (or to taste)
- 2 tablespoons olive oil (optional, for browning)
- Fresh cilantro, chopped (for garnish)
- Tortillas, rice, or beans (for serving)

COOKING INSTRUCTIONS

1. Lightly grease the inside of the slow cooker or simply add the ingredients directly.
2. For added flavor, heat olive oil in a skillet over medium-high heat. Season the pork with salt and pepper, then brown it on all sides for 4-5 minutes per side. This step is optional but adds depth of flavor. Transfer the browned pork to the slow cooker.
3. Add the chopped onion, minced garlic, diced tomatoes, orange juice, and lime juice to the slow cooker. Sprinkle the chili powder, cumin, smoked paprika, oregano, salt, and pepper over the pork.
4. Cover the slow cooker with the lid and cook on low heat for 8-10 hours or high heat for 4-6 hours, until the pork is tender and easily pulled apart with a fork.
5. Once the pork is cooked and tender, remove it from the slow cooker and place it on a cutting board. Use two forks to shred the pork into bite-sized pieces. Return the shredded pork to the slow cooker and stir it into the sauce.
6. Taste the pulled pork and adjust the seasoning with more salt, pepper, or lime juice if needed.

SERVING TIPS AND VARIATIONS

- Serve this Mexican-style pulled pork with tortillas for tacos or burritos, or use it as a filling for enchiladas or quesadillas. It also pairs well with rice, beans, or a side of Mexican corn salad.
- For extra heat, add chopped jalapeños or a pinch of cayenne pepper to the spice mix.
- Use chicken thighs instead of pork for a lighter option.
- Add 1/4 cup of tequila or beer along with the orange juice for a deeper flavor.
- Top the pulled pork with pickled onions, fresh avocado, or cotija cheese for a more authentic Mexican experience.
- If you want a crispier texture, transfer the pulled pork to a baking sheet and broil it in the oven for 3-4 minutes before serving.

MEAT AND POULTRY
2. BEEF IN MUSTARD HONEY SAUCE

- Preparation Time: 15 minutes
- Cooking Time: 6-8 hours on low or 4-5 hours on high
- Servings: 6

INGREDIENTS

- 2 pounds beef stew meat or chuck roast, cut into bite-sized pieces
- 2 tablespoons Dijon mustard
- 2 tablespoons whole grain mustard
- 3 tablespoons honey
- 1 large onion, chopped
- 3 cloves garlic, minced
- 1 cup beef broth
- 2 tablespoons olive oil (optional, for browning)
- 1 teaspoon dried thyme
- 1 tablespoon soy sauce
- 1 tablespoon balsamic vinegar (optional, for tang)
- Salt and pepper to taste
- Fresh parsley, chopped (for garnish)

COOKING INSTRUCTIONS

1. Lightly grease the inside of the slow cooker or add the ingredients directly.
2. For added flavor, heat olive oil in a skillet over medium-high heat. Season the beef with salt and pepper, then brown it in batches for 4-5 minutes until seared on all sides. This step is optional but adds depth of flavor. Transfer the browned beef to the slow cooker.
3. In the same skillet, sauté the chopped onion and garlic for about 3-4 minutes until softened. Transfer the onions and garlic to the slow cooker.
4. In a small bowl, whisk together the Dijon mustard, whole grain mustard, honey, soy sauce, balsamic vinegar (if using), and beef broth. Pour the sauce over the beef and onions in the slow cooker.
5. Sprinkle the dried thyme over the mixture and stir everything together. Season with additional salt and pepper if needed.
6. Cover the slow cooker and cook on low heat for 6-8 hours or high heat for 4-5 hours, until the beef is tender and the sauce has thickened slightly.
7. Before serving, taste the sauce and adjust seasoning with more honey for sweetness or mustard for extra tang.

SERVING TIPS AND VARIATIONS

- This flavorful beef pairs perfectly with mashed potatoes, buttered noodles, or roasted vegetables. It can also be served with crusty bread to soak up the sauce.
- For a richer sauce, add a splash of cream or stir in a tablespoon of butter during the last 15 minutes of cooking.
- Add vegetables like carrots, potatoes, or green beans to make the stew heartier.
- If you prefer a spicier version, add a pinch of red pepper flakes or a spoonful of whole grain mustard with horseradish.

MEAT AND POULTRY
3. BEEF STEWED WITH POTATOES AND CARROTS

- Preparation Time: 15 minutes
- Cooking Time: 6-8 hours on low or 4-5 hours on high
- Servings: 6

INGREDIENTS

- 2 pounds beef stew meat or chuck roast, cut into bite-sized pieces
- 4 medium potatoes, peeled and chopped
- 3 large carrots, peeled and chopped
- 1 large onion, chopped
- 3 cloves garlic, minced
- 3 cups beef broth
- 2 tablespoons tomato paste
- 1 tablespoon Worcestershire sauce
- 1 teaspoon dried thyme
- 1 teaspoon smoked paprika
- 1 bay leaf
- 2 tablespoons olive oil (optional, for browning)
- Salt and pepper to taste
- Fresh parsley, chopped (for garnish)

COOKING INSTRUCTIONS

1. Lightly grease the inside of the slow cooker or simply add the ingredients directly.
2. For added flavor, heat olive oil in a skillet over medium-high heat. Season the beef with salt and pepper, then brown it in batches for 4-5 minutes on all sides. This step is optional but enhances the flavor. Transfer the browned beef to the slow cooker.
3. In the same skillet, sauté the chopped onion and garlic for 3-4 minutes until softened. This step is optional but enhances the flavor. Transfer the onions and garlic to the slow cooker.
4. Add the chopped potatoes and carrots to the slow cooker.
5. In a small bowl, whisk together the beef broth, tomato paste, Worcestershire sauce, thyme, smoked paprika, and a pinch of salt and pepper. Pour the mixture over the beef and vegetables in the slow cooker.
6. Add the bay leaf to the slow cooker, then stir everything together.
7. Cover the slow cooker with the lid and cook on low heat for 6-8 hours or high heat for 4-5 hours, until the beef is tender and the vegetables are cooked through.
8. Before serving, remove the bay leaf. Taste the stew and adjust seasoning with more salt, pepper, or Worcestershire sauce if needed.

SERVING TIPS AND VARIATIONS

- Serve this hearty stew with warm crusty bread, mashed potatoes, or buttered noodles for a comforting meal. You can also serve it with a side of rice or quinoa.
- Add other vegetables like peas, parsnips, or celery for more variety.
- For a richer flavor, substitute part of the beef broth with red wine.
- Stir in a tablespoon of balsamic vinegar or Dijon mustard for extra depth of flavor.

MEAT AND POULTRY
4. SPICY LAMB CURRY

- Preparation Time: 20 minutes
- Cooking Time: 6-8 hours on low or 4-5 hours on high
- Servings: 6

INGREDIENTS

- 2 pounds lamb shoulder or leg, cut into bite-sized pieces
- 1 large onion, finely chopped, 4 cloves garlic, minced
- 1 tablespoon fresh ginger, grated
- 2-3 tablespoons curry powder (adjust to taste)
- 1 tablespoon garam masala
- 1 teaspoon cumin seeds, 1 teaspoon turmeric powder
- 1 teaspoon ground coriander
- 1 teaspoon chili powder (optional for extra heat)
- 1 can (14.5 oz) diced tomatoes
- 1 can (14 oz) coconut milk, 1 cup lamb or chicken broth
- 2 tablespoons tomato paste
- 1-2 green chilies, chopped (optional)
- 2 tablespoons olive oil (optional, for browning)
- Salt and pepper to taste
- Fresh cilantro, chopped (for garnish)
- Cooked rice or naan (for serving)

COOKING INSTRUCTIONS

1. Lightly grease the inside of the slow cooker or add the ingredients directly.
2. For added flavor, heat olive oil in a skillet over medium-high heat. Season the lamb with salt and pepper, then brown it in batches for 4-5 minutes until seared on all sides. This step is optional but adds depth of flavor. Transfer the browned lamb to the slow cooker.
3. In the same skillet, sauté the chopped onion, garlic, and ginger for 4-5 minutes until softened. This step enhances the curry's flavor. Transfer the mixture to the slow cooker.
4. Add the curry powder, garam masala, cumin seeds, turmeric, ground coriander, and chili powder (if using) to the slow cooker. Stir everything together to evenly coat the lamb and onions with the spices.
5. Pour the diced tomatoes, coconut milk, and broth into the slow cooker. Stir in the tomato paste and chopped green chilies (if using). Season with salt and pepper to taste.
6. Cover the slow cooker with the lid and cook on low heat for 6-8 hours or high heat for 4-5 hours, until the lamb is tender and the sauce has thickened slightly.
7. Before serving, taste the curry and adjust seasoning with more salt, pepper, or spices if needed. For extra richness, stir in a tablespoon of butter or cream at the end.

SERVING TIPS AND VARIATIONS

- This spicy lamb curry pairs well with basmati rice, naan, or roti. Add a side of cucumber raita or a fresh salad to balance the heat.
- For a milder curry, reduce the amount of chili powder and omit the green chilies.
- Add vegetables like potatoes, spinach, or bell peppers during the last hour of cooking for more texture and flavor.
- Substitute lamb with chicken thighs or beef for different variations.

MEAT AND POULTRY
5. PORK WITH PINEAPPLES AND SOY SAUCE

- Preparation Time: 15 minutes
- Cooking Time: 6-8 hours on low or 4-5 hours on high
- Servings: 6

INGREDIENTS

- 2 pounds pork shoulder or pork loin, cut into bite-sized pieces
- 1 can (20 oz) pineapple chunks, drained (reserve the juice)
- 1/2 cup soy sauce
- 1/4 cup pineapple juice (from the canned pineapples)
- 1/4 cup brown sugar
- 1 tablespoon rice vinegar (or apple cider vinegar)
- 1 tablespoon fresh ginger, minced
- 3 cloves garlic, minced
- 1 tablespoon cornstarch (optional, for thickening)
- 1 tablespoon olive oil (optional, for browning)
- 1 teaspoon chili flakes (optional, for heat)
- 1/2 teaspoon black pepper
- Fresh green onions or cilantro, chopped (for garnish)
- Cooked rice (for serving)

COOKING INSTRUCTIONS

1. Lightly grease the inside of the slow cooker or add the ingredients directly.
2. For added flavor, heat olive oil in a skillet over medium-high heat. Season the pork with black pepper, then brown it in batches for 4-5 minutes until seared on all sides. This step is optional but adds depth of flavor. Transfer the browned pork to the slow cooker.
3. In the same skillet, sauté the minced garlic and ginger for 1-2 minutes until fragrant. Transfer to the slow cooker.
4. In a small bowl, whisk together the soy sauce, pineapple juice, brown sugar, rice vinegar, and chili flakes (if using). Pour the sauce over the pork in the slow cooker.
5. Add the drained pineapple chunks to the slow cooker, distributing them evenly over the pork.
6. Cover the slow cooker and cook on low heat for 6-8 hours or high heat for 4-5 hours, until the pork is tender and fully cooked.
7. If you prefer a thicker sauce, mix 1 tablespoon of cornstarch with 2 tablespoons of water to create a slurry. Stir the slurry into the slow cooker during the last 30 minutes of cooking, allowing the sauce to thicken.
8. Before serving, taste the sauce and adjust seasoning with more soy sauce, vinegar, or sugar as needed.

SERVING TIPS AND VARIATIONS

- This dish pairs beautifully with steamed jasmine or basmati rice. You can also serve it with quinoa or noodles for a different twist.
- Add bell peppers, carrots, or broccoli during the last hour of cooking for extra color and texture.
- Use chicken thighs or beef strips as a substitute for pork.
- For a spicier version, add more chili flakes or sliced fresh chili peppers.

MEAT AND POULTRY
6. CHICKEN WITH HONEY AND MUSTARD

- **Preparation Time:** 10 minutes
- **Cooking Time:** 4-6 hours on low or 2-3 hours on high
- **Servings:** 4-6

INGREDIENTS

- 4 boneless, skinless chicken breasts (or thighs)
- 1/3 cup Dijon mustard
- 1/3 cup honey
- 2 tablespoons whole grain mustard
- 2 tablespoons olive oil
- 2 cloves garlic, minced
- 1 tablespoon apple cider vinegar (or lemon juice)
- 1 teaspoon dried thyme
- Salt and pepper to taste
- Fresh parsley, chopped (for garnish)
- Cooked rice, quinoa, or mashed potatoes (for serving)

COOKING INSTRUCTIONS

1. Lightly grease the inside of the slow cooker or add the ingredients directly.
2. In a small bowl, whisk together the Dijon mustard, whole grain mustard, honey, olive oil, minced garlic, apple cider vinegar, thyme, salt, and pepper. Mix until well combined.
3. Place the chicken breasts (or thighs) in the slow cooker. Pour the honey mustard sauce over the chicken, making sure the chicken is fully coated with the sauce.
4. Cover the slow cooker with the lid and cook on low heat for 4-6 hours or high heat for 2-3 hours, until the chicken is fully cooked and tender.
5. Once the chicken is done, if the sauce seems too thin, you can thicken it by removing the chicken and allowing the sauce to cook uncovered for an additional 15-20 minutes, or by stirring in a cornstarch slurry (1 tablespoon cornstarch mixed with 1 tablespoon water).

SERVING TIPS AND VARIATIONS

- This dish pairs well with a variety of sides, including steamed vegetables, roasted carrots, or a fresh salad. You can also serve it with crusty bread to soak up the flavorful sauce.
- Add vegetables like carrots, broccoli, or green beans to the slow cooker for a one-pot meal.
- Use chicken thighs for a juicier and richer flavor.
- For extra heat, add a pinch of red pepper flakes or a dash of hot sauce to the honey mustard sauce.
- Substitute the apple cider vinegar with lemon juice for a more citrusy flavor.
- For a creamier sauce, stir in a splash of heavy cream or Greek yogurt just before serving.

THE SUPER EASY SLOW COOKER COOKBOOK

FISH AND SEAFOOD

1. STEWED FISH WITH VEGETABLES
2. SALMON STEW IN CREAMY DILL SAUCE
3. COD STEW WITH TOMATOES AND OLIVES
4. TROUT STEW WITH LEMON AND HERBS
5. STEWED FISH IN COCONUT MILK WITH CURRY
6. SHRIMP STEW IN CREAMY GARLIC SAUCE

FISH AND SEAFOOD
1. STEWED FISH WITH VEGETABLES

- Preparation Time: 15 minutes
- Cooking Time: 3-4 hours on low or 1.5-2 hours on high
- Servings: 4-6

INGREDIENTS

- 1.5 pounds (700g) firm white fish fillets (such as cod, haddock, or tilapia), cut into pieces
- 2 medium carrots, sliced
- 1 large bell pepper, chopped
- 1 zucchini, sliced
- 1 onion, chopped
- 3 cloves garlic, minced
- 1 can (14.5 oz) diced tomatoes with their juices
- 1/2 cup vegetable or fish broth
- 2 tablespoons olive oil
- 1 teaspoon dried thyme
- 1 teaspoon dried oregano
- 1/2 teaspoon paprika
- Salt and pepper to taste
- Fresh parsley or cilantro for garnish (optional)
- Lemon wedges for serving (optional)

COOKING INSTRUCTIONS

1. Lightly grease the inside of the slow cooker with olive oil or cooking spray.
2. Add the sliced carrots, bell pepper, zucchini, onion, and minced garlic to the slow cooker. Drizzle the olive oil over the vegetables and season with salt, pepper, thyme, oregano, and paprika. Toss everything together to evenly distribute the seasoning.
3. Pour the diced tomatoes (with their juices) and vegetable or fish broth over the vegetables. Stir gently to combine.
4. Place the fish fillets on top of the vegetable mixture. Season the fish with a little salt and pepper. The fish will cook gently on top of the vegetables and absorb their flavors.
5. Cover the slow cooker and cook on low heat for 3-4 hours or high heat for 1.5-2 hours, until the fish is cooked through and flakes easily with a fork, and the vegetables are tender.
6. Before serving, taste the stew and adjust the seasoning with more salt, pepper, or herbs if needed.
7. Serve the stewed fish with vegetables in bowls, garnished with fresh parsley or cilantro. Add a squeeze of fresh lemon juice for brightness.

SERVING TIPS AND VARIATIONS

- This dish pairs well with rice, quinoa, or crusty bread to soak up the flavorful broth. You can also serve it with a light green salad or roasted potatoes.
- Use different vegetables like potatoes, green beans, or spinach for variety.
- Substitute the white fish with salmon or trout for a richer flavor.
- Add a pinch of red pepper flakes for a bit of heat, or stir in some olives for a Mediterranean twist.
- For a creamier version, stir in a tablespoon of cream or coconut milk at the end of cooking.
- If using frozen fish fillets, thaw them before adding to the slow cooker for even cooking.

FISH AND SEAFOOD
2. SALMON STEW IN CREAMY DILL SAUCE

- Preparation Time: 10 minutes
- Cooking Time: 2-3 hours on low or 1-1.5 hours on high
- Servings: 4

INGREDIENTS

- 4 salmon fillets (about 1.5 pounds/700g)
- 1 cup heavy cream (or half-and-half for a lighter option)
- 1/2 cup vegetable or fish broth
- 2 tablespoons fresh dill, chopped (or 1 teaspoon dried dill)
- 1 tablespoon lemon juice
- 2 cloves garlic, minced
- 1 small onion, finely chopped
- 1 tablespoon Dijon mustard
- 2 tablespoons butter
- Salt and pepper to taste
- Fresh dill or lemon wedges for garnish (optional)

COOKING INSTRUCTIONS

1. Lightly grease the inside of the slow cooker with butter or cooking spray.
2. In a small bowl, mix the heavy cream, vegetable or fish broth, chopped dill, lemon juice, minced garlic, Dijon mustard, and a pinch of salt and pepper. Whisk until well combined.
3. Add the chopped onion and butter to the bottom of the slow cooker. Place the salmon fillets on top of the onions. Pour the creamy dill sauce over the salmon fillets, making sure they are fully covered.
4. Cover the slow cooker and cook on low heat for 2-3 hours or high heat for 1-1.5 hours, until the salmon is cooked through and flakes easily with a fork.
5. Once done, carefully remove the salmon fillets from the slow cooker and spoon the creamy dill sauce over the top. Garnish with extra fresh dill and serve with lemon wedges for a bright, fresh flavor.

SERVING TIPS AND VARIATIONS

- Serve the stewed salmon with creamy dill sauce over rice, quinoa, or mashed potatoes. It also pairs well with steamed vegetables like asparagus, green beans, or broccoli.
- Add baby potatoes or carrots to the slow cooker to create a complete one-pot meal.
- Substitute salmon with trout or cod for a different flavor profile.
- For a dairy-free option, use coconut cream instead of heavy cream.
- Add a splash of white wine to the sauce for a richer flavor.
- If you prefer a thicker sauce, stir in 1 teaspoon of cornstarch dissolved in 1 tablespoon of water during the last 30 minutes of cooking.

FISH AND SEAFOOD
3. COD STEW WITH TOMATOES AND OLIVES

- Preparation Time: 10 minutes
- Cooking Time: 2-3 hours on low or 1-1.5 hours on high
- Servings: 4

INGREDIENTS

- 1.5 pounds (700g) cod fillets, cut into large pieces
- 1 can (14.5 oz) diced tomatoes (with juices)
- 1/2 cup pitted green or black olives, halved
- 1 small onion, chopped
- 2 cloves garlic, minced
- 1/2 cup vegetable or fish broth
- 1 tablespoon olive oil
- 1 teaspoon dried oregano
- 1 teaspoon smoked paprika
- 1/4 teaspoon red pepper flakes (optional)
- Salt and pepper to taste
- Fresh parsley, chopped (for garnish)
- Lemon wedges for serving (optional)

COOKING INSTRUCTIONS

1. Lightly grease the inside of the slow cooker with olive oil or cooking spray.
2. Add the chopped onion, minced garlic, diced tomatoes (with their juices), olives, oregano, smoked paprika, and red pepper flakes (if using) to the slow cooker. Stir to combine. Pour in the vegetable or fish broth and season with salt and pepper.
3. Place the cod fillets on top of the tomato and olive mixture. Season the fish lightly with salt and pepper.
4. Cover the slow cooker and cook on low heat for 2-3 hours or high heat for 1-1.5 hours, until the cod is cooked through and flakes easily with a fork.
5. Taste the sauce and adjust seasoning if needed. Carefully remove the cod fillets and serve them with the tomato and olive sauce. Garnish with freshly chopped parsley and a squeeze of lemon juice for brightness.

SERVING TIPS AND VARIATIONS

- Serve this stewed cod with crusty bread, couscous, rice, or quinoa to soak up the flavorful tomato and olive sauce. A side of roasted vegetables or a green salad complements the dish well.
- Use other firm white fish like haddock, halibut, or pollock instead of cod.
- Add sliced bell peppers, zucchini, or spinach for extra vegetables.
- Replace olives with capers for a tangy flavor.
- For a Mediterranean twist, stir in some crumbled feta cheese just before serving.
- To make the dish spicier, increase the amount of red pepper flakes or add a fresh chili pepper to the mix.

FISH AND SEAFOOD
4. TROUT STEW WITH LEMON AND HERBS

- Preparation Time: 10 minutes
- Cooking Time: 2-3 hours on low or 1-1.5 hours on high
- Servings: 4 servings

INGREDIENTS

- 4 trout fillets (about 1.5 pounds/700g)
- 2 lemons (one sliced, one juiced)
- 3 cloves garlic, minced
- 1/2 cup vegetable or fish broth
- 1 tablespoon olive oil
- 2 tablespoons fresh parsley, chopped
- 2 tablespoons fresh dill, chopped
- 1 teaspoon dried thyme (or 2 sprigs fresh thyme)
- Salt and pepper to taste
- Fresh herbs for garnish (optional)

COOKING INSTRUCTIONS

1. Lightly grease the inside of the slow cooker with olive oil or cooking spray.
2. Place the lemon slices at the bottom of the slow cooker. Lay the trout fillets on top of the lemon slices. Season the trout with salt, pepper, minced garlic, thyme, and half of the fresh parsley and dill.
3. Pour the vegetable or fish broth and the juice of one lemon over the trout fillets.
4. Cover the slow cooker and cook on low heat for 2-3 hours or high heat for 1-1.5 hours, until the trout is cooked through and flakes easily with a fork.
5. Carefully remove the trout fillets from the slow cooker, drizzle them with the cooking juices, and garnish with the remaining fresh herbs. Serve with extra lemon wedges if desired.

SERVING TIPS AND VARIATIONS

- Serve the stewed trout with a side of steamed vegetables, roasted potatoes, or rice. A light salad with vinaigrette pairs well with this dish.
- Use other herbs like basil, oregano, or tarragon to change the flavor profile.
- Add vegetables like asparagus, zucchini, or green beans to the slow cooker for a one-pot meal.
- Swap trout with other fish like salmon or haddock for a different taste.
- For a richer sauce, stir in a tablespoon of butter or cream at the end of cooking.
- Add a touch of white wine to the broth for a deeper flavor.

FISH AND SEAFOOD
5. STEWED FISH IN COCONUT MILK WITH CURRY

- Preparation Time: 15 minutes
- Cooking Time: 3-4 hours on low or 1.5-2 hours on high
- Servings: 4

INGREDIENTS

- 1.5 pounds (700g) firm white fish (cod, tilapia, or snapper), cut into large pieces
- 1 can (13.5 oz) coconut milk
- 1/2 cup fish or vegetable broth
- 2 tablespoons curry powder (or to taste)
- 1 tablespoon fresh ginger, grated
- 2 cloves garlic, minced, 1 small onion, chopped
- 1 red bell pepper, sliced
- 1 zucchini, sliced
- 1 tablespoon lime juice
- 2 tablespoons fresh cilantro, chopped (optional, for garnish)
- 1 tablespoon olive oil
- Salt and pepper to taste
- Red pepper flakes (optional, for heat)
- Cooked rice for serving

COOKING INSTRUCTIONS

1. Lightly grease the inside of the slow cooker with olive oil or cooking spray.
2. For extra flavor, sauté the chopped onion, garlic, and ginger in olive oil for 3-4 minutes until softened. Then transfer them to the slow cooker.
3. Place the bell pepper and zucchini slices at the bottom of the slow cooker. These will act as a base for the fish.
4. In a medium bowl, whisk together the coconut milk, fish or vegetable broth, curry powder, lime juice, and a pinch of salt and pepper. Pour this mixture over the vegetables.
5. Place the fish pieces on top of the vegetables and gently press them down so they are submerged in the curry sauce.
6. Cover the slow cooker and cook on low heat for 3-4 hours or high heat for 1.5-2 hours, until the fish is tender and flakes easily with a fork, and the vegetables are soft.
7. Serve the stewed fish in coconut milk over cooked rice, garnished with fresh cilantro and a sprinkle of red pepper flakes if you like some heat.

SERVING TIPS AND VARIATIONS

- Serve with steamed jasmine or basmati rice, quinoa, or even naan bread to soak up the flavorful coconut curry sauce.
- Use different vegetables like eggplant, carrots, or green beans to add variety.
- Replace white fish with salmon or shrimp for a richer taste.
- Add a tablespoon of fish sauce or soy sauce for an umami kick.
- To make the dish spicier, increase the amount of curry powder or add fresh chilies to the sauce.
- Stir in spinach or kale during the last 15 minutes of cooking for extra greens.

FISH AND SEAFOOD
6. SHRIMP STEW IN CREAMY GARLIC SAUCE

- Preparation Time: 10 minutes
- Cooking Time: 1-2 hours on low
- Servings: 4

INGREDIENTS

- 1.5 pounds (700g) large shrimp, peeled and deveined
- 1 cup heavy cream (or half-and-half for a lighter version)
- 1/2 cup chicken or vegetable broth
- 4 cloves garlic, minced
- 1 small onion, finely chopped
- 2 tablespoons butter
- 1 tablespoon olive oil
- 1 tablespoon lemon juice
- 1 teaspoon dried thyme (or 2 sprigs fresh thyme)
- Salt and pepper to taste
- Fresh parsley, chopped (for garnish)
- Grated Parmesan cheese (optional, for garnish)
- Lemon wedges for serving

COOKING INSTRUCTIONS

1. Lightly grease the inside of the slow cooker with olive oil or butter to prevent sticking.
2. For added flavor, melt the butter and olive oil in a skillet over medium heat. Add the minced garlic and chopped onion, sautéing for 3-4 minutes until softened. Transfer the garlic and onion mixture to the slow cooker.
3. Pour the heavy cream and chicken or vegetable broth into the slow cooker. Stir in the lemon juice, thyme, and a pinch of salt and pepper.
4. Place the shrimp into the slow cooker, making sure they are fully submerged in the creamy sauce.
5. Cover the slow cooker and cook on low heat for 1-2 hours. The shrimp will cook quickly, so check them after the first hour. They should be pink and opaque, with a tender texture. Avoid overcooking to prevent them from becoming tough.
6. Once the shrimp are cooked, stir the sauce and check the seasoning. Adjust salt, pepper, or lemon juice to taste. Garnish with chopped parsley and grated Parmesan cheese if desired. Serve with lemon wedges for added brightness.

SERVING TIPS AND VARIATIONS

- Serve the creamy garlic shrimp over pasta, rice, or mashed potatoes for a rich and satisfying meal. A side of crusty bread is perfect for dipping into the sauce.
- Add a pinch of red pepper flakes or cayenne pepper for a spicy kick.
- For a lighter version, substitute the heavy cream with coconut milk.
- Stir in spinach or kale during the last 10-15 minutes of cooking for added greens.
- Use seafood mix (shrimp, scallops, mussels) instead of just shrimp for a more varied dish.
- For extra richness, stir in a tablespoon of cream cheese or grated Parmesan at the end of cooking.

THE SUPER EASY SLOW COOKER COOKBOOK

VEGETABLES AND SIDES

1. STEWED POTATOES WITH CARROTS AND ONIONS
2. MASHED POTATOES WITH GARLIC AND CREAM
3. PUMPKIN AND SPINACH STEW
4. STEWED CAULIFLOWER WITH CHEESE
5. BUCKWHEAT PORRIDGE WITH VEGETABLES
6. RICE WITH VEGETABLES AND SPICES

VEGETABLES AND SIDES
1. STEWED POTATOES WITH CARROTS AND ONIONS

- Preparation Time: 15 minutes
- Cooking Time: 4-6 hours on low or 2-3 hours on high
- Servings: 4-6

INGREDIENTS

- 6 medium potatoes, peeled and chopped into bite-sized pieces
- 3 medium carrots, peeled and sliced
- 1 large onion, chopped
- 3 cloves garlic, minced
- 1 cup vegetable or chicken broth
- 2 tablespoons olive oil or butter
- 1 teaspoon dried thyme (or 1 tablespoon fresh thyme)
- 1 teaspoon dried parsley (or 1 tablespoon fresh parsley)
- Salt and pepper to taste
- Fresh parsley for garnish (optional)

COOKING INSTRUCTIONS

1. Lightly grease the inside of the slow cooker with olive oil or butter.
2. Add the chopped potatoes, sliced carrots, and chopped onion to the slow cooker. Sprinkle the minced garlic on top.
3. Drizzle the olive oil (or melted butter) over the vegetables. Add the thyme, parsley, salt, and pepper to taste. Toss the vegetables lightly to coat them with the oil and seasoning.
4. Pour the vegetable or chicken broth into the slow cooker. The broth will help the vegetables to cook evenly and become tender.
5. Cover the slow cooker and cook on low heat for 4-6 hours or high heat for 2-3 hours, until the potatoes and carrots are tender but not mushy.
6. Once the vegetables are cooked, carefully stir them in the slow cooker to distribute the flavors. Garnish with fresh parsley if desired, and serve hot.

SERVING TIPS AND VARIATIONS

- This stewed vegetable dish can be served as a side dish to grilled or roasted meats, or enjoyed as a simple vegetarian main course. It pairs well with crusty bread, rice, or quinoa.
- For added richness, stir in 1/4 cup of heavy cream or milk at the end of cooking.
- Add other vegetables like celery, bell peppers, or green beans to the slow cooker for extra color and flavor.
- For a heartier meal, add chunks of chicken, sausage, or beef to the slow cooker.
- You can also sprinkle grated cheese (like Parmesan or cheddar) on top before serving for an extra layer of flavor.
- A splash of lemon juice or vinegar before serving can brighten the flavors of the dish.

VEGETABLES AND SIDES
2. MASHED POTATOES WITH GARLIC AND CREAM

- Preparation Time: 10 minutes
- Cooking Time: 4 hours on low or 2 hours on high
- Servings: 6-8

INGREDIENTS

- 3 pounds (1.4 kg) russet or Yukon gold potatoes, peeled and cut into chunks
- 6 cloves garlic, minced
- 1 cup heavy cream
- 1/2 cup unsalted butter, cut into pieces
- 1/2 cup milk (more if needed)
- Salt and pepper to taste
- Fresh parsley or chives for garnish (optional)

COOKING INSTRUCTIONS

1. Lightly grease the inside of the slow cooker with butter or cooking spray.
2. Place the peeled and chopped potatoes into the slow cooker. Add the minced garlic and a pinch of salt and pepper.
3. Place the butter pieces on top of the potatoes. Pour in the heavy cream, ensuring the potatoes are partially covered.
4. Cover the slow cooker and cook on low heat for 4 hours or high heat for 2 hours, until the potatoes are tender and easily pierced with a fork.
5. Once the potatoes are fully cooked, use a potato masher or an electric hand mixer to mash them directly in the slow cooker. Gradually add the milk to achieve your desired consistency. Season with additional salt and pepper to taste.
6. Garnish with fresh parsley or chives if desired. Serve the mashed potatoes hot as a side dish.

SERVING TIPS AND VARIATIONS

- These mashed potatoes are perfect alongside roast chicken, turkey, or beef, or as part of a holiday meal.
- For a richer flavor, replace some of the milk with sour cream or cream cheese.
- Add a handful of grated Parmesan or cheddar cheese for cheesy mashed potatoes.
- To make the dish more savory, mix in crispy bacon bits or sautéed onions.
- You can adjust the garlic flavor by roasting the garlic before adding it to the slow cooker for a more mellow, sweet taste.
- If you prefer a lighter version, replace heavy cream with half-and-half or just use more milk.

VEGETABLES AND SIDES
3. PUMPKIN AND SPINACH STEW

- Preparation Time: 15 minutes
- Cooking Time: 4-6 hours on low or 2-3 hours on high
- Servings: 4-6

INGREDIENTS

- 4 cups pumpkin, peeled and cut into cubes (or butternut squash)
- 4 cups fresh spinach (or 2 cups frozen spinach, thawed)
- 1 onion, chopped
- 3 cloves garlic, minced
- 1 can (14.5 oz) diced tomatoes
- 1 cup vegetable broth
- 1 teaspoon ground cumin
- 1/2 teaspoon ground cinnamon
- 1/2 teaspoon paprika
- Salt and pepper to taste
- 2 tablespoons olive oil
- 1/4 cup coconut milk (optional, for a creamier texture)
- Fresh cilantro for garnish (optional)

COOKING INSTRUCTIONS

1. Lightly grease the inside of the slow cooker with olive oil.
2. Place the cubed pumpkin (or butternut squash), chopped onion, and minced garlic in the slow cooker. Add the diced tomatoes (with juice), vegetable broth, cumin, cinnamon, paprika, salt, and pepper.
3. Cover the slow cooker and cook on low heat for 4-6 hours or high heat for 2-3 hours, until the pumpkin is tender but not mushy.
4. In the last 20-30 minutes of cooking, add the fresh spinach to the slow cooker. Stir to combine, allowing the spinach to wilt and blend into the stew.
5. For a creamier texture, stir in the coconut milk during the last 10 minutes of cooking.
6. Once the stew is done cooking, taste and adjust the seasoning if needed. Garnish with fresh cilantro and serve hot.

SERVING TIPS AND VARIATIONS

- This stew pairs well with rice, quinoa, or couscous. You can also serve it with crusty bread for a more filling meal.
- Add chickpeas or lentils for extra protein and heartiness.
- For a spicier version, add a pinch of cayenne pepper or red chili flakes.
- You can substitute kale or Swiss chard for spinach if desired.
- For a richer flavor, sauté the onions and garlic in olive oil before adding them to the slow cooker.
- You can also add a tablespoon of tomato paste for a deeper tomato flavor.

VEGETABLES AND SIDES
4. STEWED CAULIFLOWER WITH CHEESE

- Preparation Time: 10 minutes
- Cooking Time: 3-4 hours on low or 1-2 hours on high
- Servings: 4-6

INGREDIENTS

- 1 large head of cauliflower, cut into florets
- 1 cup shredded cheddar cheese (or any preferred cheese)
- 1/2 cup heavy cream (or milk)
- 1/2 cup vegetable or chicken broth
- 2 tablespoons butter
- 2 cloves garlic, minced
- 1/2 teaspoon ground paprika
- Salt and pepper to taste
- Fresh parsley for garnish (optional)
- 1/4 cup grated Parmesan cheese (optional, for extra flavor)

COOKING INSTRUCTIONS

1. Lightly grease the inside of the slow cooker with butter or cooking spray.
2. Place the cauliflower florets into the slow cooker. Sprinkle the minced garlic over the top.
3. In a small bowl, whisk together the heavy cream (or milk) and vegetable or chicken broth. Pour this mixture over the cauliflower.
4. Sprinkle the shredded cheddar cheese evenly over the cauliflower. Add the butter, breaking it into small pieces and scattering them over the top. Season with paprika, salt, and pepper.
5. Cover the slow cooker and cook on low heat for 3-4 hours or high heat for 1-2 hours, until the cauliflower is tender but not mushy and the cheese is melted.
6. In the last 30 minutes of cooking, sprinkle grated Parmesan cheese over the top for an extra layer of flavor.
7. Once the cauliflower is tender, give it a gentle stir to mix the cheese and sauce. Garnish with fresh parsley and serve hot.

SERVING TIPS AND VARIATIONS

- Serve this cheesy cauliflower as a side dish with roasted meats, grilled chicken, or fish. It also works well as a low-carb vegetarian main dish.
- Add cooked bacon bits or ham to the slow cooker for a heartier, more savory dish.
- For a crunchy topping, add breadcrumbs or crushed crackers during the last 30 minutes of cooking.
- For extra creaminess, stir in a tablespoon of cream cheese or sour cream when adding the cheddar cheese.
- You can also substitute broccoli or mix it with the cauliflower for added variety.
- For a sharper cheese flavor, try using a combination of cheddar and Gruyère cheese.

VEGETABLES AND SIDES
5. BUCKWHEAT PORRIDGE WITH VEGETABLES

- Preparation Time: 10 minutes
- Cooking Time: 2-3 hours on low or 1-1.5 hours on high
- Servings: 4-6

INGREDIENTS

- 1 cup buckwheat groats, rinsed
- 2 cups vegetable broth (or water)
- 1 medium onion, chopped
- 2 medium carrots, diced
- 1 bell pepper, chopped
- 1 zucchini, diced
- 2 cloves garlic, minced
- 2 tablespoons olive oil
- 1 teaspoon dried thyme or oregano
- Salt and pepper to taste
- Fresh parsley for garnish (optional)

COOKING INSTRUCTIONS

1. Lightly grease the inside of the slow cooker with olive oil or cooking spray.
2. For extra flavor, heat olive oil in a skillet over medium heat. Sauté the chopped onions, carrots, bell pepper, and garlic for 3-4 minutes until they soften slightly. This step is optional but adds a richer flavor to the dish.
3. Place the rinsed buckwheat groats, sautéed (or raw) vegetables, zucchini, and minced garlic into the slow cooker. Pour in the vegetable broth or water.
4. Add the dried thyme (or oregano), salt, and pepper to taste. Stir the ingredients to combine evenly.
5. Cover the slow cooker and cook on low heat for 2-3 hours or high heat for 1-1.5 hours, until the buckwheat is tender and has absorbed most of the liquid, and the vegetables are cooked through.
6. Once the buckwheat is cooked, give it a stir to fluff the grains and combine the vegetables evenly. Taste and adjust seasoning if needed. Garnish with fresh parsley if desired, and serve hot.

SERVING TIPS AND VARIATIONS

- This buckwheat porridge can be served as a hearty vegetarian main dish or as a side dish with grilled meats, fish, or tofu. It also pairs well with a simple salad or pickled vegetables.
- Add other vegetables such as mushrooms, spinach, or peas for variety.
- For a heartier dish, stir in cooked chickpeas or beans for added protein.
- Add a tablespoon of soy sauce or balsamic vinegar during the last 10 minutes of cooking for extra flavor.
- Top the porridge with grated cheese or a dollop of sour cream for a creamy finish.
- You can make it spicy by adding a pinch of red pepper flakes or cayenne pepper.
- For a richer texture, stir in a tablespoon of butter or olive oil before serving.

VEGETABLES AND SIDES
6. RICE WITH VEGETABLES AND SPICES

- Preparation Time: 10 minutes
- Cooking Time: 2-3 hours on low or 1-1.5 hours on high
- Servings: 4-6

INGREDIENTS

- 1 cup long-grain rice (basmati or jasmine), rinsed
- 2 cups vegetable broth (or water)
- 1 onion, chopped
- 1 carrot, diced
- 1 bell pepper, chopped
- 1 zucchini, diced
- 1 cup peas (fresh or frozen)
- 2 cloves garlic, minced
- 2 tablespoons olive oil
- 1 teaspoon ground cumin
- 1/2 teaspoon turmeric
- 1/2 teaspoon ground coriander
- 1/2 teaspoon paprika
- Salt and pepper to taste
- Fresh cilantro or parsley for garnish (optional)

COOKING INSTRUCTIONS

1. Lightly grease the inside of the slow cooker with olive oil or cooking spray.
2. For a richer flavor, heat olive oil in a skillet over medium heat. Sauté the onion, carrot, bell pepper, and garlic for 3-4 minutes until slightly softened. This step enhances the flavor but can be skipped if preferred.
3. Place the rinsed rice, sautéed (or raw) vegetables, peas, and zucchini into the slow cooker.
4. Add the ground cumin, turmeric, coriander, paprika, salt, and pepper to the slow cooker. Pour in the vegetable broth or water, and stir to combine everything evenly.
5. Cover the slow cooker and cook on low heat for 2-3 hours or high heat for 1-1.5 hours, until the rice is tender and has absorbed the liquid, and the vegetables are cooked through.
6. Once the rice is cooked, fluff it with a fork to separate the grains. Taste and adjust the seasoning if necessary. Garnish with fresh cilantro or parsley before serving.

SERVING TIPS AND VARIATIONS

- Serve the rice as a main dish or as a side dish with grilled chicken, tofu, or fish. It pairs well with yogurt or a fresh salad.
- Add diced tomatoes or corn for extra color and flavor.
- You can substitute the peas with chickpeas or lentils for added protein.
- For a spicy version, add a pinch of red pepper flakes or cayenne pepper.
- Mix in cooked sausage, shrimp, or tofu during the last 10 minutes of cooking for a heartier dish.
- To give the dish a Mediterranean twist, add olives and a squeeze of lemon juice before serving.
- If you want a richer flavor, use coconut milk instead of vegetable broth for a creamy, tropical version of the dish.

54 THE SUPER EASY SLOW COOKER COOKBOOK

BEANS AND GRAINS

1. BEANS STEWED WITH TOMATOES AND GARLIC
2. BARLEY PORRIDGE WITH MUSHROOMS
3. CHICKPEAS WITH VEGETABLES AND SPICES
4. RED BEANS WITH SMOKED SAUSAGE
5. OATMEAL WITH APPLES AND CINNAMON
6. LENTILS WITH TOMATOES AND SPINACH

BEANS AND GRAINS
1. BEANS STEWED WITH TOMATOES AND GARLIC

- Preparation Time: 10 minutes
- Cooking Time: 6-8 hours on low or 3-4 hours on high
- Servings: 4-6

INGREDIENTS

- 2 cans (15 oz each) cannellini beans or navy beans, drained and rinsed
- 4 large tomatoes, chopped (or 1 can diced tomatoes)
- 4 cloves garlic, minced
- 1 onion, chopped
- 2 tablespoons olive oil
- 1 teaspoon dried oregano
- 1 teaspoon dried thyme
- Salt and pepper to taste
- 1/2 teaspoon red pepper flakes (optional, for heat)
- 1/2 cup vegetable broth or water
- Fresh parsley or basil for garnish (optional)

COOKING INSTRUCTIONS

1. Lightly grease the inside of the slow cooker with olive oil or cooking spray.
2. Place the drained beans, chopped tomatoes, minced garlic, chopped onion, oregano, thyme, salt, pepper, and red pepper flakes (if using) into the slow cooker. Pour the vegetable broth or water over the mixture and stir to combine.
3. Cover the slow cooker and cook on low heat for 6-8 hours or high heat for 3-4 hours, until the beans are tender and the flavors have melded together.
4. Once the beans are cooked, taste and adjust the seasoning if needed. Add more salt, pepper, or red pepper flakes according to your preference.
5. Garnish the beans with fresh parsley or basil before serving. Serve the dish warm.

SERVING TIPS AND VARIATIONS

- Serve the stewed beans as a main dish with crusty bread, or as a side dish with grilled meats or fish. They also pair well with rice, quinoa, or couscous.
- Add chopped bell peppers or zucchini for more vegetables.
- Stir in fresh spinach or kale during the last 30 minutes of cooking for added greens.
- For a smoky flavor, add a teaspoon of smoked paprika or use fire-roasted tomatoes.
- If you prefer a creamier texture, stir in a tablespoon of tomato paste or a splash of heavy cream.
- For added protein, mix in cooked sausage or bacon before serving.
- Use different types of beans, such as black beans, kidney beans, or pinto beans, for variety.

BEANS AND GRAINS
2. BARLEY PORRIDGE WITH MUSHROOMS

- Preparation Time: 10 minutes
- Cooking Time: 4-5 hours on low or 2-3 hours on high
- Servings: 4-6

INGREDIENTS

- 1 1/2 cups pearl barley, rinsed
- 2 cups mushrooms, sliced (any variety: button, cremini, or shiitake)
- 1 onion, chopped
- 3 cloves garlic, minced
- 1 tablespoon olive oil
- 4 cups vegetable or chicken broth
- 1 teaspoon dried thyme
- Salt and pepper to taste
- 1/4 cup grated Parmesan cheese (optional, for garnish)
- Fresh parsley or chives for garnish (optional)

COOKING INSTRUCTIONS

1. Lightly grease the inside of the slow cooker with olive oil or cooking spray.
2. For extra flavor, heat olive oil in a skillet over medium heat. Sauté the onions, garlic, and mushrooms for 5-7 minutes until softened and slightly browned. This step can be skipped if you're short on time.
3. Place the rinsed barley, sautéed mushrooms, onions, and garlic (or raw if skipping the sauté step) into the slow cooker. Add the dried thyme, salt, and pepper, then pour in the vegetable or chicken broth.
4. Cover the slow cooker and cook on low heat for 4-5 hours or high heat for 2-3 hours, until the barley is tender and has absorbed most of the broth.
5. Once the porridge is ready, taste and adjust the seasoning as needed. Serve hot, garnished with grated Parmesan cheese and fresh parsley or chives if desired.

SERVING TIPS AND VARIATIONS

- Serve this hearty barley porridge as a main dish or a side. It pairs well with roasted vegetables or grilled meats, and can also be enjoyed on its own as a warm, comforting meal.
- Add diced carrots, celery, or zucchini for extra vegetables.
- For a creamier texture, stir in a splash of cream or a tablespoon of butter just before serving.
- Use wild or mixed mushrooms for a more earthy flavor.
- For added protein, stir in cooked sausage, bacon, or tofu.
- You can also top the dish with a fried or poached egg for a complete meal.

BEANS AND GRAINS
3. CHICKPEAS WITH VEGETABLES AND SPICES

- Preparation Time: 10 minutes
- Cooking Time: 6-8 hours on low or 3-4 hours on high
- Servings: 4-6

INGREDIENTS

- 2 cans (15 oz each) chickpeas, drained and rinsed (or 1 1/2 cups dried chickpeas, soaked overnight)
- 1 zucchini, diced
- 2 carrots, 1 bell pepper, 1 onion, chopped
- 3 cloves garlic, minced
- 1 can (15 oz) diced tomatoes
- 1 teaspoon ground cumin
- 1 teaspoon ground coriander
- 1/2 teaspoon turmeric
- 1/2 teaspoon smoked paprika
- 1/4 teaspoon ground cinnamon
- Salt and pepper to taste
- 1/2 teaspoon red pepper flakes (optional, for heat)
- 2 cups vegetable broth
- 2 tablespoons olive oil
- Fresh cilantro or parsley for garnish (optional)

COOKING INSTRUCTIONS

1. Lightly grease the inside of the slow cooker with olive oil or cooking spray.
2. Place the drained chickpeas (or soaked chickpeas if using dried), zucchini, carrots, bell pepper, onion, garlic, and diced tomatoes into the slow cooker.
3. Sprinkle the cumin, coriander, turmeric, smoked paprika, cinnamon, salt, pepper, and red pepper flakes (if using) over the vegetables and chickpeas. Pour in the vegetable broth and stir everything to combine.
4. Cover the slow cooker and cook on low heat for 6-8 hours or high heat for 3-4 hours, until the vegetables are tender and the chickpeas are fully cooked.
5. Once the dish is ready, taste and adjust the seasoning if necessary. Serve hot, garnished with fresh cilantro or parsley for added flavor and color.

SERVING TIPS AND VARIATIONS

- Serve this chickpea and vegetable dish over rice, quinoa, or couscous for a complete meal. You can also enjoy it with a side of warm flatbread or naan.
- Add diced sweet potatoes or cauliflower for more hearty vegetables.
- For added protein, stir in cooked chicken or tofu.
- If using dried chickpeas, ensure they are soaked overnight and increase the broth by 1 cup for proper cooking.
- If you prefer a more saucy consistency, add a can of coconut milk or extra diced tomatoes.
- Top with a dollop of yogurt for a creamy finish and serve with lemon wedges for a fresh touch.

BEANS AND GRAINS
4. RED BEANS WITH SMOKED SAUSAGE

- Preparation Time: 15 minutes
- Cooking Time: 6-8 hours on low or 4-5 hours on high
- Servings: 6

INGREDIENTS

- 1 lb (450 g) dried red beans, soaked overnight
- 12 oz (340 g) smoked sausage, sliced
- 1 onion, chopped
- 3 cloves garlic, minced
- 1 bell pepper, chopped
- 2 celery stalks, chopped
- 1 teaspoon smoked paprika
- 1 teaspoon dried thyme
- 1/2 teaspoon cayenne pepper (optional for heat)
- 1 bay leaf
- Salt and pepper to taste
- 4 cups chicken or vegetable broth
- 1 tablespoon olive oil
- Fresh parsley for garnish (optional)
- Cooked rice for serving

COOKING INSTRUCTIONS

1. Lightly grease the inside of the slow cooker with olive oil or cooking spray.
2. For extra flavor, you can sauté the sliced smoked sausage in a skillet over medium heat for 4-5 minutes, until lightly browned. This step is optional but enhances the taste.
3. Place the soaked red beans, sliced sausage, chopped onion, garlic, bell pepper, and celery into the slow cooker. Add the smoked paprika, thyme, cayenne pepper (if using), bay leaf, salt, and pepper.
4. Pour the chicken or vegetable broth over the ingredients, ensuring the beans are fully covered by the liquid. Stir everything to combine.
5. Cover the slow cooker and cook on low heat for 6-8 hours or high heat for 4-5 hours, until the beans are tender and the flavors have melded together.
6. Once the red beans and sausage are cooked, taste and adjust the seasoning if necessary. Remove the bay leaf before serving. Garnish with fresh parsley and serve over cooked rice.

SERVING TIPS AND VARIATIONS

- Serve this dish over white rice or brown rice for a classic pairing. It can also be served with cornbread or crusty bread on the side.
- For added richness, stir in a spoonful of butter or olive oil before serving.
- You can add diced tomatoes or a splash of tomato sauce for a slightly tangier flavor.
- To make the dish spicier, increase the cayenne pepper or add sliced jalapeños.
- For a more traditional Cajun flavor, add 1/2 teaspoon of Creole or Cajun seasoning.
- Use andouille sausage for a spicier, more flavorful result.
- If you prefer a creamier texture, mash a small portion of the beans with a spoon before serving.

BEANS AND GRAINS
5. OATMEAL WITH APPLES AND CINNAMON

- Preparation Time: 10 minutes
- Cooking Time: 6-8 hours on low or 3-4 hours on high
- Servings: 4-6

INGREDIENTS

- 2 cups old-fashioned oats
- 2 apples, peeled, cored, and chopped
- 4 cups milk (or a mix of milk and water for a lighter option)
- 1/4 cup brown sugar or maple syrup (adjust to taste)
- 1 teaspoon ground cinnamon
- 1/4 teaspoon ground nutmeg (optional)
- 1/4 teaspoon salt
- 1 teaspoon vanilla extract
- 1 tablespoon butter (optional for richness)
- Toppings: chopped nuts, additional cinnamon, honey, or fresh fruit (optional)

COOKING INSTRUCTIONS

1. Lightly grease the inside of the slow cooker with butter or cooking spray to prevent sticking.
2. In the slow cooker, add the oats, chopped apples, milk (or milk and water combination), brown sugar, cinnamon, nutmeg (if using), salt, and vanilla extract. Stir everything together to combine.
3. Cover the slow cooker and cook on low heat for 6-8 hours (overnight for a warm breakfast) or high heat for 3-4 hours. The oats should be tender, and the apples will soften.
4. Once cooked, stir the oatmeal to mix in any liquid that may have settled on the top. If the oatmeal is too thick, you can add a bit more milk to reach your desired consistency. Serve warm.
5. Garnish with your favorite toppings such as chopped nuts, a drizzle of honey or maple syrup, a sprinkle of additional cinnamon, or fresh fruit.

SERVING TIPS AND VARIATIONS

- Serve this oatmeal as a hearty and healthy breakfast. You can refrigerate leftovers for up to 3 days and reheat with a splash of milk.
- Nutty Oatmeal: Add 1/4 cup of chopped walnuts, pecans, or almonds during the last hour of cooking for a crunchy texture.
- Creamy Version: Stir in 1/4 cup of cream or coconut milk during the last 30 minutes of cooking for a richer texture.
- Fruit Options: Swap the apples for pears or peaches, or mix in dried fruit like raisins or cranberries for variety.
- Spiced Oatmeal: For a spicier flavor, add a pinch of ground cloves or ginger.
- Protein Boost: Stir in a tablespoon of peanut butter or almond butter just before serving for added protein and creaminess.
- Low-Sugar Option: Omit the brown sugar or maple syrup and rely on the natural sweetness of the apples.

BEANS AND GRAINS
6. LENTILS WITH TOMATOES AND SPINACH

- Preparation Time: 10 minutes
- Cooking Time: 4-6 hours on low or 2-3 hours on high
- Servings: 4-6

INGREDIENTS

- 1 1/2 cups dried green or brown lentils, rinsed
- 1 can (14.5 oz) diced tomatoes
- 4 cups vegetable broth (or water)
- 1 onion, finely chopped
- 3 cloves garlic, minced
- 2 carrots, diced
- 1 teaspoon ground cumin
- 1/2 teaspoon ground coriander
- 1/2 teaspoon turmeric
- Salt and pepper to taste
- 4 cups fresh spinach, roughly chopped
- 1 tablespoon olive oil
- Fresh lemon juice (optional, for serving)
- Fresh parsley or cilantro for garnish (optional)

COOKING INSTRUCTIONS

1. Lightly grease the inside of the slow cooker with olive oil or cooking spray.
2. Place the rinsed lentils, diced tomatoes (with their juices), vegetable broth, chopped onion, garlic, carrots, cumin, coriander, turmeric, salt, and pepper into the slow cooker. Stir everything to combine.
3. Cover the slow cooker and cook on low heat for 4-6 hours or high heat for 2-3 hours, until the lentils are tender and the flavors have melded together.
4. About 10-15 minutes before serving, stir in the chopped spinach. Allow it to wilt into the stew as it finishes cooking.
5. Taste the lentils and adjust the seasoning if needed. For a fresh, tangy flavor, squeeze a little lemon juice over the top before serving. Garnish with fresh parsley or cilantro if desired.

SERVING TIPS AND VARIATIONS

- Serve this lentil dish as a main course or side dish. It pairs well with crusty bread, rice, or quinoa. You can also top it with a dollop of yogurt for extra creaminess.
- Protein Boost: Add cooked chicken, tofu, or chickpeas for extra protein.
- Creamy Version: Stir in 1/4 cup coconut milk during the last 10 minutes of cooking for a creamy, rich texture.
- Spice it up: Add a pinch of red pepper flakes or cayenne pepper for a bit of heat.
- Herb Variations: Swap out spinach for kale or Swiss chard, or use a mix of fresh herbs like thyme, oregano, or basil.
- Vegetable Add-Ins: Feel free to add other vegetables such as diced zucchini, bell peppers, or potatoes.

THE SUPER EASY SLOW COOKER COOKBOOK

SAUCES AND DIPS

1. TOMATO SAUCE WITH BASIL
2. BARBECUE SAUCE
3. CHEDDAR CHEESE SAUCE
4. SPICY TOMATO SAUCE WITH CHILI PEPPERS
5. CURRY SAUCE WITH COCONUT MILK
6. MARINARA SAUCE WITH TOMATOES AND HERBS

SAUCES AND DIPS
1. TOMATO SAUCE WITH BASIL

- Preparation Time: 10 minutes
- Cooking Time: 4-6 hours on low or 2-3 hours on high
- Servings: 6-8

INGREDIENTS

- 2 (28 oz) cans crushed tomatoes (or 6-8 large fresh tomatoes, chopped)
- 1 small onion, finely chopped
- 4 garlic cloves, minced
- 1/4 cup olive oil
- 1 teaspoon sugar (optional)
- 1 teaspoon salt (or to taste)
- 1/2 teaspoon black pepper
- 1 teaspoon dried oregano
- 1/4 teaspoon red pepper flakes (optional)
- 1/2 cup fresh basil leaves, torn or chopped
- 2 tablespoons tomato paste (optional, for richer flavor)
- 1 bay leaf
- Freshly grated Parmesan cheese (optional for serving)

COOKING INSTRUCTIONS

1. Lightly grease the inside of the slow cooker with olive oil or use cooking spray to prevent sticking.
2. For enhanced flavor, you can sauté the chopped onion and garlic in a small pan with olive oil over medium heat until softened and fragrant, about 3-4 minutes. This step is optional but adds a depth of flavor.
3. In the slow cooker, combine the crushed tomatoes (or fresh tomatoes), sautéed onion and garlic (if you sautéed them), olive oil, sugar, salt, pepper, oregano, red pepper flakes (if using), and bay leaf. Stir well to combine.
4. Cover and cook on low heat for 4-6 hours or high heat for 2-3 hours. Stir occasionally, especially in the last hour, to prevent burning and ensure even cooking.
5. About 30 minutes before the sauce is done, stir in the fresh basil leaves. This will infuse the sauce with its fragrant flavor without losing the bright basil aroma.
6. Once the sauce is cooked, remove the bay leaf and taste the sauce. Adjust seasoning with additional salt, pepper, or sugar if needed.
7. Serve the tomato sauce over pasta, as a pizza sauce, or as a base for other dishes. Garnish with freshly grated Parmesan cheese if desired.

SERVING TIPS AND VARIATIONS

- This tomato sauce pairs perfectly with pasta, gnocchi, or as a topping for pizzas, lasagna, or stuffed vegetables. It can also be used as a dipping sauce for breadsticks or garlic bread.
- Chunky Sauce: Add chopped bell peppers, mushrooms, or zucchini to the sauce for added texture and nutrients.
- Creamy Version: Stir in 1/2 cup of heavy cream or a spoonful of ricotta cheese at the end for a creamy tomato sauce.

SAUCES AND DIPS
2. BARBECUE SAUCE

- Preparation Time: 5-10 minutes
- Cooking Time: 2-3 hours on low
- Servings: 3 cups (approximately 12 servings)

INGREDIENTS

- 2 cups ketchup
- 1/2 cup apple cider vinegar
- 1/4 cup Worcestershire sauce
- 1/4 cup brown sugar
- 1/4 cup honey or molasses
- 2 tablespoons Dijon mustard
- 2 tablespoons soy sauce
- 1 tablespoon smoked paprika
- 1 teaspoon garlic powder
- 1 teaspoon onion powder
- 1/2 teaspoon black pepper
- 1/2 teaspoon cayenne pepper (optional, for heat)
- 1/2 teaspoon liquid smoke (optional, for smoky flavor)
- Salt to taste

COOKING INSTRUCTIONS

1. Lightly grease the inside of the slow cooker with cooking spray or olive oil to prevent sticking.
2. In the slow cooker, whisk together the ketchup, apple cider vinegar, Worcestershire sauce, brown sugar, honey (or molasses), Dijon mustard, soy sauce, smoked paprika, garlic powder, onion powder, black pepper, and cayenne pepper (if using). Stir until all the ingredients are well combined.
3. Cover the slow cooker and cook on low heat for 2-3 hours, stirring occasionally. The sauce will thicken as it cooks and the flavors will meld together.
4. After cooking, taste the sauce and adjust the seasoning if necessary. Add more salt, pepper, or cayenne if you want more heat. If the sauce is too thick, you can thin it with a bit of water or apple cider vinegar.
5. If you want a smoky flavor, stir in the liquid smoke during the last 30 minutes of cooking.
6. Once the sauce is done, let it cool. Transfer the sauce to an airtight container and store it in the refrigerator for up to 2 weeks.

SERVING TIPS AND VARIATIONS

- This barbecue sauce is perfect for slathering on ribs, chicken, pork, or beef. You can use it as a marinade, baste during grilling, or serve it as a dipping sauce.
- Sweeter Version: Add more brown sugar or honey for a sweeter sauce.
- Tangy Twist: For a tangier sauce, increase the amount of apple cider vinegar.
- Spicier Sauce: Add more cayenne pepper, chili flakes, or even a splash of hot sauce for extra heat.
- Fruit-Infused BBQ Sauce: Stir in some puréed pineapple, peaches, or mango for a fruity variation.
- Smokier Flavor: Add more liquid smoke or use smoked paprika for a stronger smoky flavor.

SAUCES AND DIPS
3. CHEDDAR CHEESE SAUCE

- Preparation Time: 5 minutes
- Cooking Time: 1-2 hours on low
- Servings: 4 cups (approximately 8 servings)

INGREDIENTS

- 2 cups shredded sharp cheddar cheese
- 1 cup whole milk
- 1/2 cup heavy cream
- 2 tablespoons unsalted butter
- 2 tablespoons all-purpose flour
- 1/2 teaspoon Dijon mustard
- 1/4 teaspoon garlic powder
- 1/4 teaspoon onion powder
- Salt and pepper to taste
- A pinch of cayenne pepper (optional, for heat)

COOKING INSTRUCTIONS

1. In a small saucepan, melt the butter over medium heat. Once melted, whisk in the flour to form a roux. Cook the roux for 1-2 minutes until it turns a light golden color, stirring constantly.
2. Transfer the roux to the slow cooker. Add the milk, heavy cream, Dijon mustard, garlic powder, onion powder, and a pinch of cayenne pepper (if using). Stir to combine.
3. Cover and cook on low heat for 1 hour, stirring occasionally to ensure the sauce remains smooth and the ingredients combine well.
4. After 1 hour, stir in the shredded cheddar cheese a little at a time, whisking constantly to melt the cheese into the sauce. Make sure the sauce is smooth and well-blended after each addition.
5. Once all the cheese is added, continue cooking for another 30 minutes on low, stirring occasionally, until the cheese sauce is fully melted, smooth, and thickened.
6. Taste the sauce and adjust seasoning with salt and pepper. If the sauce is too thick, you can thin it by stirring in additional milk, a tablespoon at a time, until the desired consistency is achieved.

SERVING TIPS AND VARIATIONS

- This cheddar cheese sauce is perfect for drizzling over vegetables, nachos, pasta, or baked potatoes. It can also be used as a dip for pretzels, fries, or chips.
- Spicy Cheese Sauce: Add chopped jalapeños or more cayenne pepper for extra heat.
- Garlic Herb Sauce: Stir in fresh chopped herbs like parsley or chives for added flavor.
- Smoky Flavor: Use smoked cheddar or add a dash of liquid smoke for a smoky twist.
- Extra Creamy Sauce: For an even richer sauce, increase the amount of heavy cream or add a small amount of cream cheese.
- Mexican Cheese Sauce: Add 1/4 teaspoon ground cumin and a bit of chili powder for a Mexican-style cheese sauce.

SAUCES AND DIPS
4. SPICY TOMATO SAUCE WITH CHILI PEPPERS

- Preparation Time: 10 minutes
- Cooking Time: 4-5 hours on low
- Servings: 6 cups (approximately 6-8 servings)

INGREDIENTS

- 2 cans (28 oz each) crushed tomatoes
- 1 medium onion, finely chopped
- 4 cloves garlic, minced
- 2-3 chili peppers (such as jalapeños or serranos), finely chopped (adjust for heat preference)
- 1 tablespoon olive oil
- 1 tablespoon tomato paste
- 1 teaspoon sugar (optional, to balance acidity)
- 1 teaspoon dried oregano
- 1 teaspoon dried basil
- 1/2 teaspoon smoked paprika
- 1/2 teaspoon ground cumin (optional, for extra depth)
- Salt and pepper to taste
- Fresh chopped parsley or cilantro for garnish (optional)

COOKING INSTRUCTIONS

1. In a skillet over medium heat, warm the olive oil. Add the chopped onions and sauté until softened, about 3-4 minutes. Add the garlic and cook for an additional minute, stirring frequently to avoid burning.
2. Transfer the sautéed onions and garlic to the slow cooker. Add the crushed tomatoes, tomato paste, chopped chili peppers, oregano, basil, smoked paprika, ground cumin (if using), and sugar (if using) to the slow cooker. Stir to combine all ingredients.
3. Cover the slow cooker and cook on low heat for 4-5 hours. Stir occasionally to ensure even cooking and prevent the sauce from sticking to the sides. The flavors will meld together, and the sauce will thicken as it cooks.
4. Taste the sauce after 3-4 hours of cooking. Adjust seasoning with salt and pepper as needed. If the sauce is too acidic, add a pinch more sugar. If you prefer more heat, add additional chopped chili peppers or a pinch of red pepper flakes.
5. For a smoother sauce, you can use an immersion blender to purée the sauce to your desired consistency, or leave it chunky if preferred.
6. Once the sauce has reached your desired thickness and flavor, turn off the slow cooker.

SERVING TIPS AND VARIATIONS

- Extra Smoky Flavor: Add more smoked paprika or a dash of liquid smoke for a deeper, smoky taste.
- Italian-Inspired: Stir in a splash of balsamic vinegar and fresh basil for an Italian twist.
- Mexican-Style: Add a pinch of ground cumin, coriander, and lime juice to give the sauce a Mexican flavor.
- Rich and Creamy: Stir in a little heavy cream or coconut milk at the end for a creamier sauce.

SAUCES AND DIPS
5. CURRY SAUCE WITH COCONUT MILK

- Preparation Time: 10 minutes
- Cooking Time: 3-4 hours on low
- Servings: 4-6 cups (approximately 6-8 servings)

INGREDIENTS

- 1 can (14 oz) coconut milk (full fat for richness)
- 1 medium onion, finely chopped
- 3 cloves garlic, minced
- 1 tablespoon fresh ginger, minced
- 2-3 tablespoons curry powder (adjust based on spice preference)
- 1 teaspoon ground turmeric
- 1/2 teaspoon ground cumin
- 1/2 teaspoon ground coriander
- 1 tablespoon tomato paste
- 1 tablespoon vegetable oil or coconut oil
- 1 teaspoon sugar (optional, to balance flavors)
- 1/2 teaspoon chili flakes or 1 chopped chili pepper (optional, for heat)
- Salt and pepper to taste
- Fresh cilantro for garnish (optional)

COOKING INSTRUCTIONS

1. Heat the oil in a skillet over medium heat. Add the chopped onions and sauté until softened, about 3-4 minutes. Add the garlic and ginger, and cook for an additional minute, stirring frequently.
2. Stir in the curry powder, turmeric, cumin, and coriander. Toast the spices in the pan for 1-2 minutes until fragrant, being careful not to burn them.
3. Transfer the onion, garlic, and spice mixture to the slow cooker. Add the coconut milk, tomato paste, sugar (if using), and chili flakes or chopped chili pepper (if using). Stir to combine all the ingredients.
4. Cover and cook on low heat for 3-4 hours. Stir occasionally to ensure even cooking and prevent the sauce from sticking to the sides. The flavors will meld together as the sauce cooks.
5. After cooking, taste the sauce and adjust the seasoning with salt and pepper. If you prefer a thicker sauce, leave the lid off for the last 30 minutes to reduce the sauce. If too thick, you can thin it out with a bit of vegetable or chicken broth.
6. Once the sauce has reached your desired thickness and flavor, turn off the slow cooker. Garnish with fresh cilantro before serving.

SERVING TIPS AND VARIATIONS

- Serve this coconut curry sauce over steamed rice, noodles, or roasted vegetables. It also pairs well with chicken, shrimp, tofu, or paneer for a complete meal.
- Spicier Version: Increase the amount of chili or add a tablespoon of Thai red curry paste for extra heat.
- Creamier Sauce: Add 1/4 cup of heavy cream or more coconut milk for a richer, creamier sauce.
- Green Curry: Use green curry paste instead of curry powder for a Thai-style green curry sauce.
- Citrus Kick: Stir in a splash of lime juice at the end for a tangy, refreshing finish.

SAUCES AND DIPS
6. MARINARA SAUCE WITH TOMATOES AND HERBS

- Preparation Time: 10 minutes
- Cooking Time: 4-6 hours on low
- Servings: 6 cups (approximately 6-8 servings)

INGREDIENTS

- 2 cans (28 oz each) crushed tomatoes
- 1 small onion, finely chopped
- 4 cloves garlic, minced
- 1 tablespoon olive oil
- 1 tablespoon tomato paste
- 1 teaspoon sugar (optional, to balance acidity)
- 1 teaspoon dried oregano
- 1 teaspoon dried basil
- 1/2 teaspoon red pepper flakes (optional, for heat)
- 1/2 teaspoon salt (or to taste)
- 1/2 teaspoon black pepper
- Fresh basil and parsley for garnish (optional)

COOKING INSTRUCTIONS

1. In a skillet, heat the olive oil over medium heat. Add the chopped onions and cook until softened, about 3-4 minutes. Add the garlic and cook for another minute until fragrant, being careful not to burn.
2. Transfer the sautéed onions and garlic to the slow cooker. Add the crushed tomatoes, tomato paste, dried oregano, dried basil, sugar (if using), salt, pepper, and red pepper flakes (if using). Stir everything together until well combined.
3. Cover the slow cooker and cook on low heat for 4-6 hours. Stir occasionally to ensure the sauce is cooking evenly and not sticking to the sides. As the sauce cooks, it will thicken and develop deeper flavors.
4. After the cooking time, taste the sauce and adjust the seasoning with more salt, pepper, or sugar if needed. If you prefer a thicker sauce, cook uncovered for the last 30 minutes to allow the sauce to reduce.
5. Once the sauce has reached your desired thickness and flavor, turn off the slow cooker. Garnish with freshly chopped basil and parsley before serving.

SERVING TIPS AND VARIATIONS

- Marinara sauce is perfect for pasta dishes, lasagna, as a pizza sauce, or as a dipping sauce for garlic bread. It can also be used as a base for stews and soups.
- Chunky Marinara: Add diced tomatoes along with crushed tomatoes for a chunkier texture.
- Roasted Veggies: Add roasted bell peppers, zucchini, or mushrooms to give the sauce more texture and depth of flavor.
- Creamy Marinara: Stir in a splash of heavy cream or coconut milk at the end for a creamier version of the sauce.

70 THE SUPER EASY SLOW COOKER COOKBOOK

DESSERTS

1. CHOCOLATE FONDANT
2. APPLE PIE
3. CARAMEL PUDDING
4. PUMPKIN PIE
5. BAKED APPLES WITH CINNAMON AND SUGAR
6. CHOCOLATE CAKE WITH CARAMEL

DESSERTS
1. CHOCOLATE FONDANT

- Preparation Time: 15 minutes
- Cooking Time: 1 hour
- Servings: 4

INGREDIENTS

- 200g dark chocolate (70% cocoa), chopped
- 100g unsalted butter, plus extra for greasing
- 2 large eggs
- 2 large egg yolks
- 100g caster sugar
- 50g all-purpose flour
- 1/2 teaspoon vanilla extract
- A pinch of salt
- Cocoa powder or flour (for dusting ramekins)

COOKING INSTRUCTIONS

1. Preheat the slow cooker on low. Grease 4 small ramekins with butter and dust them lightly with cocoa powder or flour, tapping out the excess.
2. In a heatproof bowl, melt the chocolate and butter together over a saucepan of simmering water (double boiler method). Stir occasionally until smooth, then remove from heat and set aside to cool slightly.
3. In a separate mixing bowl, whisk together the eggs, egg yolks, and sugar until the mixture becomes pale and fluffy. This should take about 3-5 minutes.
4. Gently fold the melted chocolate mixture into the egg mixture using a spatula. Be careful not to deflate the air in the eggs. Sift the flour and a pinch of salt into the mixture, folding it in carefully. Add the vanilla extract and stir until everything is just combined.
5. Divide the mixture evenly between the greased ramekins. The ramekins should be about 3/4 full to allow room for the fondants to rise.
6. Place the ramekins inside the slow cooker. Add enough hot water to the slow cooker to come halfway up the sides of the ramekins. Cover with the slow cooker lid and cook on low for about 1 hour, or until the edges are firm but the centers remain soft and molten.
7. Once cooked, remove the ramekins from the slow cooker carefully. Let them sit for 2-3 minutes before gently running a knife around the edges to loosen the fondants. Invert each ramekin onto a serving plate and lift it off to reveal the molten center.

SERVING TIPS AND VARIATIONS

- Serve your Chocolate Fondant with a scoop of vanilla ice cream or a dollop of whipped cream for a perfect balance of warm and cold textures.
- You can add a teaspoon of espresso powder or orange zest to the chocolate mixture for an extra layer of flavor.

DESSERTS
2. APPLE PIE

- Preparation Time: 20 minutes
- Cooking Time: 2-3 hours
- Servings: 6-8

INGREDIENTS

- 6 medium apples (Granny Smith, Honeycrisp, or any tart variety), peeled, cored, and sliced
- 1 tablespoon lemon juice
- 1/2 cup granulated sugar
- 1/4 cup brown sugar
- 1 tablespoon cinnamon
- 1/2 teaspoon nutmeg
- 1/4 teaspoon ground cloves (optional)
- 1 tablespoon all-purpose flour
- 1 tablespoon cornstarch
- 1 pre-made pie crust (or homemade)
- 1 tablespoon butter, cut into small pieces
- 1 egg (for egg wash)
- 1 tablespoon water (for egg wash)

COOKING INSTRUCTIONS

1. In a large mixing bowl, combine the sliced apples, lemon juice, granulated sugar, brown sugar, cinnamon, nutmeg, ground cloves (if using), flour, and cornstarch. Toss everything together until the apples are evenly coated with the mixture. Set aside.
2. Lightly grease the inside of the slow cooker with butter or cooking spray.
3. Roll out the pie crust and fit it into the bottom of the slow cooker. Gently press the crust up the sides, making sure it covers the bottom evenly. You can leave a bit of crust hanging over the edge.
4. Pour the apple mixture into the slow cooker on top of the pie crust. Dot the filling with small pieces of butter to add richness.
5. If desired, you can add a top layer of pie crust, either by laying it flat or making a lattice pattern. Press the edges of the top and bottom crusts together to seal the pie.
6. In a small bowl, whisk the egg with 1 tablespoon of water to make an egg wash. Brush this over the top crust to give it a nice golden color when it cooks.
7. Cover the slow cooker with a clean kitchen towel (to prevent condensation from dripping onto the pie) and place the lid over the towel. Cook on low for 2-3 hours, or until the apples are tender and the crust is golden.
8. Once the pie is cooked, carefully lift it out of the slow cooker using the edges of the parchment paper. Let it cool slightly before slicing and serving.

SERVING TIPS AND VARIATIONS

- Serve your Apple Pie warm with a scoop of vanilla ice cream or a dollop of whipped cream for a classic pairing.
- Add 1/4 cup of chopped nuts like walnuts or pecans for extra crunch. You can also drizzle some caramel sauce over the top before serving for a richer flavor.

THE SUPER EASY SLOW COOKER COOKBOOK

DESSERTS
3. CARAMEL PUDDING

- Preparation Time: 15 minutes
- Cooking Time: 2-3 hours
- Servings: 6

INGREDIENTS

- 1/2 cup granulated sugar
- 2 tablespoons water
- 1 tablespoon butter
- 1/4 cup heavy cream

- 3 cups whole milk
- 4 large eggs
- 1/2 cup granulated sugar
- 1 teaspoon vanilla extract
- A pinch of salt

COOKING INSTRUCTIONS

1. In a small saucepan over medium heat, combine the granulated sugar and water. Cook without stirring until the sugar melts and turns a deep amber color, about 5-7 minutes. Swirl the pan gently to ensure even caramelization.
2. Remove from heat and carefully whisk in the butter and heavy cream. Pour the caramel into a heatproof dish or ramekins, dividing evenly if using multiple dishes.
3. In a mixing bowl, whisk together the milk, eggs, sugar, vanilla extract, and a pinch of salt until well combined. Make sure the sugar is fully dissolved.
4. Gently pour the pudding mixture over the caramel in the ramekins or heatproof dish. Cover each ramekin with aluminum foil to prevent condensation from affecting the pudding.
5. Place a small rack or folded kitchen towel in the bottom of your slow cooker to keep the ramekins elevated. Arrange the ramekins on top of the rack. Fill the slow cooker with hot water until it reaches halfway up the sides of the ramekins.
6. Cover the slow cooker with the lid and cook on low for 2-3 hours, or until the pudding is set but still slightly jiggly in the center. The cooking time may vary depending on the size of the ramekins or dish.
7. Once the pudding is cooked, carefully remove the ramekins from the slow cooker. Let them cool to room temperature, then refrigerate for at least 2 hours (or overnight) to allow the pudding to set fully.
8. To serve, run a knife around the edges of each pudding, then invert the ramekin onto a serving plate, allowing the caramel sauce to pool over the top.

SERVING TIPS AND VARIATIONS

- This caramel pudding is delicious on its own, but for added indulgence, you can serve it with a dollop of whipped cream or fresh berries on the side.

DESSERTS
4. PUMPKIN PIE

- Preparation Time: 15 minutes
- Cooking Time: 3-4 hours
- Servings: 8

INGREDIENTS

- 1 1/2 cups graham cracker crumbs or crushed digestive biscuits
- 1/4 cup granulated sugar
- 1/2 cup unsalted butter, melted
- 2 cups pumpkin purée (canned or homemade)
- 1 cup evaporated milk
- 2 large eggs
- 1/2 cup granulated sugar
- 1/4 cup brown sugar
- 1 teaspoon vanilla extract
- 1 teaspoon ground cinnamon
- 1/2 teaspoon ground ginger
- 1/4 teaspoon ground cloves
- 1/4 teaspoon ground nutmeg
- A pinch of salt

COOKING INSTRUCTIONS

1. In a medium bowl, combine the graham cracker crumbs, granulated sugar, and melted butter. Stir until the mixture resembles wet sand.
2. Press the mixture firmly into the bottom of a lightly greased slow cooker, forming an even layer. Use a flat-bottomed glass to help compact the crust.
3. In a large mixing bowl, whisk together the pumpkin purée, evaporated milk, eggs, granulated sugar, brown sugar, vanilla extract, cinnamon, ginger, cloves, nutmeg, and a pinch of salt until smooth and well combined.
4. Carefully pour the pumpkin mixture over the prepared crust in the slow cooker, spreading it evenly with a spatula.
5. Cover the slow cooker with the lid, place a towel under the lid to catch condensation, and cook on low for 3-4 hours, or until the filling is set and a knife inserted into the center comes out mostly clean. The edges of the pie should be firm, and the center may be slightly soft but will set further as it cools.
6. Turn off the slow cooker and let the pie cool in the cooker for about 30 minutes. Carefully remove the inner pot from the slow cooker and let it cool to room temperature.
7. Once the pie has cooled, transfer it to the refrigerator and chill for at least 2 hours, or preferably overnight, to fully set the filling.

SERVING TIPS AND VARIATIONS

- Whipped cream or a dollop of vanilla ice cream complements the flavors of pumpkin pie beautifully.
- For a different twist, use crushed ginger snaps or Oreo cookies in place of graham crackers for the crust.
- Feel free to adjust the spices to your liking or use a pre-mixed pumpkin pie spice if you prefer.

DESSERTS
5. BAKED APPLES WITH CINNAMON AND SUGAR

- Preparation Time: 10 minutes
- Cooking Time: 2-3 hours
- Servings: 4-6

INGREDIENTS

- 4-6 medium-sized apples (Granny Smith, Honeycrisp, or any baking apple)
- 1/4 cup brown sugar
- 1 teaspoon ground cinnamon
- 1/4 teaspoon ground nutmeg (optional)
- 1/4 cup chopped walnuts or pecans (optional)
- 1/4 cup raisins or dried cranberries (optional)
- 1 tablespoon butter, cut into small cubes
- 1/2 cup apple juice or water

COOKING INSTRUCTIONS

1. Core the apples, leaving the bottom intact to create a well for the filling. You can use a corer or a small knife. Peel a strip of skin from the top of each apple to prevent splitting.
2. In a small bowl, combine the brown sugar, cinnamon, nutmeg (if using), chopped nuts, and raisins or dried cranberries (if desired).
3. Fill the cored apples with the sugar mixture. Press the mixture down into the well of each apple. Top each apple with a small cube of butter.
4. Place the apples in the slow cooker, standing upright. Pour the apple juice or water around the apples to help them cook and prevent sticking.
5. Cover the slow cooker with the lid and cook on low for 2-3 hours, or until the apples are tender but still holding their shape. Check for doneness by inserting a fork into the apples; they should be soft but not mushy.
6. Carefully remove the apples from the slow cooker using a spoon or spatula. Serve warm, spooning some of the liquid from the bottom of the slow cooker over the apples for extra flavor.

SERVING TIPS AND VARIATIONS

- Top the baked apples with whipped cream, vanilla ice cream, or a drizzle of caramel sauce for an extra indulgent dessert.
- Add a pinch of ground ginger or cloves to the sugar mixture for a spicier version. You can also replace the apple juice with orange juice for a citrusy twist.
- Store leftover baked apples in an airtight container in the refrigerator for up to 3 days. Reheat in the microwave before serving.

DESSERTS
6. CHOCOLATE CAKE WITH CARAMEL

- Preparation Time: 20 minutes
- Cooking Time: 2-3 hours
- Servings: 8-10

INGREDIENTS

- 1 1/4 cups all-purpose flour
- 1 cup granulated sugar
- 1/2 cup unsweetened cocoa powder
- 1 1/2 teaspoons baking powder
- 1/2 teaspoon baking soda
- 1/4 teaspoon salt
- 2 large eggs
- 1/2 cup vegetable oil
- 1 teaspoon vanilla extract
- 1 cup milk
- 1/2 cup hot water
- 1 cup caramel sauce (store-bought or homemade)
- 1/4 cup heavy cream (optional for extra creaminess)

COOKING INSTRUCTIONS

1. Grease the bottom and sides of your slow cooker with butter or non-stick spray. You can also line it with parchment paper to make removal easier.
2. In a large bowl, whisk together flour, sugar, cocoa powder, baking powder, baking soda, and salt until well combined.
3. In a separate bowl, whisk together the eggs, vegetable oil, and vanilla extract. Add the milk and mix until smooth.
4. Slowly add the wet ingredients into the dry mixture and stir until well combined.
5. Add the hot water and mix until the batter is smooth. The batter will be thin.
6. If desired, mix the caramel sauce with heavy cream for a creamier texture. Set aside.
7. Pour half of the chocolate batter into the prepared slow cooker.
8. Drizzle half of the caramel sauce over the batter.
9. Pour the remaining chocolate batter on top, followed by the rest of the caramel sauce. Gently swirl the caramel with a knife or spatula to create a marbled effect.
10. Cover the slow cooker with a lid and cook on low for 2-3 hours. The cake is done when a toothpick inserted into the center comes out clean or with a few moist crumbs.
11. If condensation forms on the lid, carefully wipe it off to avoid water dripping onto the cake.
12. Once done, turn off the slow cooker and allow the cake to cool for 10-15 minutes before removing it from the slow cooker. Transfer to a cooling rack and let it cool completely.
13. Serve the cake warm, drizzled with extra caramel sauce or topped with a scoop of vanilla ice cream.

78 THE SUPER EASY SLOW COOKER COOKBOOK

DRINKS

1. MULLED WINE
2. HOT CHOCOLATE
3. PUMPKIN SPICE LATTE
4. GINGER TEA WITH LEMON
5. STRAWBERRY CIDER WITH MINT
6. SPICED MILK TEA

DRINKS
1. MULLED WINE

- Preparation Time: 10 minutes
- Cooking Time: 1-2 hours
- Servings: 6-8

INGREDIENTS

- 1 bottle (750 ml) red wine (Merlot, Cabernet, or any dry red wine)
- 1/4 cup brandy (optional for extra warmth)
- 1/4 cup honey or sugar (adjust to taste)
- 1 orange, sliced
- 1 lemon, sliced (optional)
- 4 cinnamon sticks
- 5-6 whole cloves
- 2-3 star anise
- 1/2 teaspoon ground nutmeg or a few whole nutmeg pieces
- 2-3 cardamom pods (optional)
- 1-2 cups water (optional, to dilute if needed)

COOKING INSTRUCTIONS

1. Set your slow cooker to low heat.
2. Pour the bottle of red wine into the slow cooker.
3. Add the sliced orange (and lemon if using), cinnamon sticks, cloves, star anise, nutmeg, and cardamom pods.
4. Stir in the honey (or sugar) until it dissolves. Add brandy if using for an extra kick.
5. Cover the slow cooker and let the mixture heat on low for 1-2 hours. The goal is to warm the wine gently without letting it boil, as boiling can affect the flavor. Stir occasionally.
6. After about 1 hour, taste the mulled wine. Adjust the sweetness by adding more honey or sugar if needed. Add water if you prefer a milder version.
7. Once the wine is heated and the flavors are well infused, turn off the slow cooker.
8. Ladle the mulled wine into mugs, making sure to include slices of orange and a cinnamon stick for garnish.

SERVING TIPS AND VARIATIONS

- Serve each cup with an extra cinnamon stick or orange peel for added flavor and presentation.
- Add a splash of apple cider for an extra fruity twist.
- Use a combination of spices like allspice or ground ginger for a unique flavor profile.
- Replace the red wine with cranberry juice, grape juice, or a non-alcoholic wine option, and reduce the honey or sugar to balance the sweetness.

DRINKS
2. HOT CHOCOLATE

- Preparation Time: 5 minutes
- Cooking Time: 2 hours
- Servings: 6-8

INGREDIENTS

- 4 cups whole milk
- 2 cups heavy cream
- 1 1/2 cups semi-sweet chocolate chips or chopped dark chocolate
- 1/4 cup cocoa powder
- 1/4 cup sugar (adjust to taste)
- 1 teaspoon vanilla extract
- Whipped cream or marshmallows (for topping)

COOKING INSTRUCTIONS

1. Set your slow cooker to low heat.
2. Pour the whole milk and heavy cream into the slow cooker.
3. Add the chocolate chips, cocoa powder, and sugar. Stir well to combine.
4. Cover the slow cooker and cook on low for about 2 hours, stirring occasionally to help the chocolate melt and blend smoothly.
5. After 1 hour, stir in the vanilla extract to enhance the flavor.
6. Keep an eye on the hot chocolate to ensure it doesn't overheat or scorch at the bottom. Stir often to maintain a creamy consistency.
7. Once the hot chocolate is smooth, creamy, and fully heated, ladle it into mugs.
8. Top with whipped cream or marshmallows for a decadent finish.

SERVING TIPS AND VARIATIONS

- Add a drizzle of chocolate syrup or a sprinkle of cocoa powder for an extra touch of chocolatey goodness.
- Add a pinch of ground cinnamon or nutmeg for a warm, spiced twist.
- For a peppermint version, stir in 1/4 teaspoon of peppermint extract or garnish with crushed candy canes.
- Substitute the milk and cream with almond milk or coconut milk for a dairy-free version of this hot chocolate.

DRINKS
3. PUMPKIN SPICE LATTE

- **Preparation Time:** 10 minutes
- **Cooking Time:** 2 hours
- **Servings:** 6-8

INGREDIENTS

- 4 cups strong brewed coffee
- 4 cups milk (whole, almond, or oat milk)
- 1/2 cup pumpkin puree
- 1/4 cup maple syrup or brown sugar (adjust to taste)
- 2 teaspoons pumpkin pie spice (or a mix of cinnamon, nutmeg, ginger, and cloves)
- 2 teaspoons vanilla extract
- Whipped cream (for garnish)
- Ground cinnamon (for garnish)

COOKING INSTRUCTIONS

1. Set your slow cooker to low heat.
2. Pour the brewed coffee, milk, pumpkin puree, maple syrup (or brown sugar), and pumpkin pie spice into the slow cooker. Stir until well combined.
3. Cover and let the mixture cook on low heat for 2 hours, stirring occasionally to ensure everything is well blended.
4. During the last 10 minutes of cooking, stir in the vanilla extract.
5. Once the latte is ready, pour it into mugs and top with whipped cream and a sprinkle of ground cinnamon for garnish.

SERVING TIPS AND VARIATIONS

- **Dairy-Free Option:** Use almond milk, coconut milk, or oat milk for a dairy-free version.
- **Sweetener Swap:** Adjust the sweetness by using honey, agave syrup, or your preferred sweetener instead of maple syrup or sugar.
- **Spiced Variation:** Add an extra dash of cinnamon or nutmeg to enhance the warming spices.
- **Stronger Coffee:** For a bolder flavor, use espresso shots instead of brewed coffee.

DRINKS
4. GINGER TEA WITH LEMON

- **Preparation Time:** 5 minutes
- **Cooking Time:** 2 hours
- **Servings:** 6-8

INGREDIENTS

- 8 cups water
- 1 large piece of fresh ginger (about 3-4 inches), sliced thinly
- 1-2 lemons, sliced
- 1/4 cup honey or to taste
- Optional: cinnamon stick or a few cloves for added flavor
- Fresh mint (for garnish, optional)

COOKING INSTRUCTIONS

1. Set your slow cooker to low heat.
2. Pour the water into the slow cooker and add the sliced ginger and lemon. If using cinnamon sticks or cloves, add them now.
3. Cover and let the tea steep on low for 2 hours, allowing the flavors to infuse into the water.
4. After the tea has brewed, stir in honey to taste, and adjust the sweetness as desired.
5. Ladle the hot ginger tea into mugs. You can garnish each mug with a slice of lemon and fresh mint, if desired.

SERVING TIPS AND VARIATIONS

- **Adjusting Strength:** For a stronger ginger flavor, you can slice the ginger thinner or let it steep for a longer time in the slow cooker.
- **Cold Version:** Let the ginger tea cool down, then refrigerate for a refreshing iced version. Serve over ice with a slice of lemon.
- **Herbal Additions:** For a more complex flavor, try adding fresh mint, turmeric, or a pinch of cayenne pepper for a bit of heat.
- **Sweetness Alternatives:** Use maple syrup, agave, or coconut sugar instead of honey, depending on your preference.

DRINKS
5. STRAWBERRY CIDER WITH MINT

- **Preparation Time:** 10 minutes
- **Cooking Time:** 2-3 hours
- **Servings:** 6-8

INGREDIENTS

- 6 cups apple cider
- 2 cups fresh or frozen strawberries, halved
- 1/4 cup honey or sugar (adjust to taste)
- 1/4 cup fresh mint leaves
- 1 cinnamon stick (optional, for added flavor)
- 1 lemon, thinly sliced
- Fresh mint sprigs (for garnish)

COOKING INSTRUCTIONS

1. Set your slow cooker to low heat.
2. Pour the apple cider into the slow cooker. Add the halved strawberries, mint leaves, lemon slices, and cinnamon stick if using.
3. Cover and let the mixture cook on low for 2-3 hours, allowing the strawberries and mint to infuse the cider with flavor. Stir occasionally.
4. After cooking, taste the cider. If it needs more sweetness, stir in honey or sugar to taste. Let it dissolve completely.
5. If you prefer a smoother drink, strain the cider to remove the strawberry pieces, mint, and lemon slices before serving.
6. Ladle the strawberry cider into mugs and garnish with fresh mint sprigs.

SERVING TIPS AND VARIATIONS

- **Cold Version:** After the cider has cooled, refrigerate and serve over ice for a refreshing summer drink. Add sparkling water for a fizzy twist.
- **Spice It Up:** For more complexity, add a few cloves or a star anise to the slow cooker along with the cinnamon stick.
- **Minty Fresh:** Adjust the mint flavor by adding more mint leaves during cooking or as a fresh garnish.
- **Strawberry-Lemon Zing:** If you want a tangier flavor, add more lemon slices or a splash of fresh lemon juice before serving.

DRINKS
6. SPICED MILK TEA

- Preparation Time: 5 minutes
- Cooking Time: 2 hours
- Servings: 4

INGREDIENTS

- 4 cups whole milk (or any milk of your choice)
- 2 cups water
- 4 black tea bags (or 4 teaspoons of loose black tea)
- 2 cinnamon sticks
- 4-6 whole cloves
- 4-6 cardamom pods, lightly crushed
- 1 teaspoon ground ginger (or 1-inch piece fresh ginger, peeled and sliced)
- 1 teaspoon vanilla extract
- 1-2 tablespoons honey or sugar (adjust to taste)
- Ground cinnamon (for garnish, optional)

COOKING INSTRUCTIONS

1. Set your slow cooker to low heat.
2. Pour the milk and water into the slow cooker. Add the tea bags, cinnamon sticks, cloves, cardamom pods, ginger, and vanilla extract.
3. Cover the slow cooker and let the tea simmer on low for 2 hours, allowing the spices to infuse into the milk. Stir occasionally.
4. After the tea has simmered, remove the tea bags and spice solids (cinnamon sticks, cardamom pods, etc.). Stir in honey or sugar to taste.
5. Ladle the spiced milk tea into mugs and sprinkle with ground cinnamon if desired.

SERVING TIPS AND VARIATIONS

- Adjust the Sweetness: Sweeten to your taste with honey, sugar, or a sweetener of your choice.
- Spice it Up: Add other spices like star anise, nutmeg, or a pinch of black pepper for an extra kick.
- Dairy-Free Option: Use almond milk, coconut milk, or any other non-dairy alternative to make this tea vegan.
- Iced Version: For a refreshing cold drink, let the spiced milk tea cool and serve over ice. You can add a splash of cold milk before serving.

CONCLUSION

This collection of recipes highlights the versatility and ease of the slow cooker, making it an invaluable tool for both beginners and experienced home cooks.

By using this method, you can save time, reduce the need for constant supervision, and still enjoy meals that are nourishing, satisfying, and full of flavor.

We hope that this cookbook has inspired you to embrace slow cooking as a way to bring comfort, flavor, and ease into your kitchen!

Thank you for choosing this book! We would love to hear your thoughts. If you have a moment, please consider leaving a review on Amazon.

Your feedback helps other readers make their choice and inspires authors to create more books!

To leave your review of a book on Amazon, please scan the QR code:

Printed in Great Britain
by Amazon